Endorsements for the Second Edition

This book is a must-read for any psychotherapist. It explores the real-world and often secret problems encountered in clinical practice in a creative, personal, and very useful fashion. In this world of increasing professional accountability and liability, clinicians can be assured that their practices will be much better off for having implemented the commonsense suggestions made by the authors.
—*Jeffrey N. Younggren, PhD, ABPP, Risk Management Consultant, American Psychological Association Insurance Trust*

This book is very readable, enjoyable, and a breath of fresh air in a field with many secrets. A glimpse into the secret, private, and unspoken world of the therapist. There is no other book like it! A delight to read.
—*John D. Robinson, EdD, MPH, ABPP, Professor of Psychiatry and Surgery, Howard University College of Medicine, Howard University Hospital, Washington, DC*

This is a very brave book. Provocative without being proscriptive, it is a must-read for all practicing clinicians and would make a superb supplemental text for graduate courses in ethics. The cases alone are well worth the price of the book!
—*Ruth E. Fassinger, PhD, Professor, Counseling Psychology, University of Maryland, College Park; Fellow, American Psychological Association*

Engaging, accessible, and gentle in tone, this book boldly addresses a number of topics that are often ignored in the training and professional development of psychologists. Its provocative observations and questions, sensitive analyses of ethical and professional problems, and practical recommendations for trainees and supervisors dealing with a range of "taboo topics" make it a unique resource.
—*Virginia Gutman, PhD, Professor and Chair, Department of Psychology, Gallaudet University, Washington, DC*

A remarkably useful work with extraordinary depth, invaluable to everyone from trainees to experienced professionals who want to prepare for pitfalls in practice as well as to do their best work. Nothing available in the professional literature can match this contribution by three leaders in the field who have provided a virtual cornucopia of useful guidance about so many vital things that are rarely discussed. An essential work for those teaching ethics or seeking to practice ethically in any mental health field, this volume has the sanguine and in-depth examination needed to truly master these issues. The most practical book on boundaries and ethics I have read in any language . . . essential for students, teachers, supervisors, and practicing clinicians. Used as a text, the book would allow one to avoid doing a syllabus for an advanced course in professional practice issues.

—*Gary R. Schoener, MEq, Licensed Psychologist, Executive Director, Walk-In Counseling Center, Minneapolis, MN*

Pope, Sonne, and Greene have written a practical, thought-provoking, and comprehensive guide to exploring the sensitive issues embedded in mental health practice. They approach this content with fearlessness, humor, and wisdom, challenging professionals to explore the real impact of our values, assumptions, and personal interests on our clients. This book is a uniquely valuable resource for faculty and clinicians committed to responsible practice.

—*Elizabeth Reynolds Welfel, PhD, Professor, Cleveland State University, Cleveland, OH*

Pope, Sonne, and Greene's new book provides an excellent resource for all mental health professionals and their trainees to examine issues that are rarely discussed in graduate programs. This clearly written book not only asks perplexing questions about various dilemmas encountered in professional practice but also provides thoughtful answers leading to ethical action. This book should be required reading in any ethics or professional issues seminar.

—*Emil Rodolfa, PhD, Director, Davis Counseling and Psychological Services, University of California, Davis; Former Chair, Association of Psychology Postdoctoral and Internship Centers; former President, State of California Board of Psychology*

This book is about those difficult, or even impossible, dilemmas and quandaries of psychotherapy—the double-binds and provocations with which our patients unexpectedly confront us. The authors gather anecdotes and scenarios from the widest spectrum of theoretical orientations and professional (or unprofessional) settings. It is an invaluable book that presents psychotherapy practice and ethics as a set of remarkably interesting questions with no easy answers.

—*Martin H. Williams, PhD, Clinical and Forensic Psychologist, San Jose, CA*

What Therapists Don't Talk About and Why is simply excellent: helpful, thoughtful, brave, entertaining, and so very "experience-near." This book addresses seemingly taboo issues (e.g., therapists' attraction to clients) in ways that can help all of us negotiate difficult, but all-too-human dilemmas in an ethical and clinically sensitive manner. Pope, Sonne, and Greene are, of course, thoroughly serious and comprehensive in their treatment of this topic; nevertheless, they are also quite humorous and cynical at appropriate times, and these qualities, in combination with multiple case examples, make this important book quite accessible. Highly recommended.

—*Barry A. Farber, PhD, Professor, Director of Clinical Training, Clinical Psychology Program, Teachers College, Columbia University, New York, NY*

Convincingly and readably, the authors show therapists how to confront their own demons of fear, anger, guilt, shame, embarrassment, prejudice, sexual arousal, immobilization, and helplessness that can arise in the therapeutic encounter and threaten to derail the process. A how-to book of extraordinary utility.

—*Elaine B. Pinderhughes, Emerita Professor, Graduate School of Social Work, Boston College, Boston, MA*

The authors roll back the carpet and help us look at what we've swept under it. They make us uncomfortable, asking personally tough questions about our feelings in clinical situations. The book is a significant advance because it goes beyond the "just don'ts" and helps us to understand what is personally challenging and learn what to do about it.

This volume will be helpful for students and practitioners alike and would be extremely valuable in peer supervision groups. Ethics educators rack their brains for ways to help improve our ethical behavior; this one goes in the toolbox.

—*Michael C. Gottlieb, PhD, ABPP, Independent Practice, Dallas, TX*

Pope, Sonne, and Greene's discerning combination of thought-provoking questions and topical client scenarios fosters the self-examination of personal and taboo topics in the clinical field. This is an enormously essential book addressing often ignored client–therapist issues; for example, a therapist's disclosure of his or her sexual orientation, fear of a violent client, a client's culture and

hygiene, and needs for a handicapped-accessible office. Both the novice and seasoned practitioner will benefit from its matter-of-fact approach as a quasi-ethical guide for enhancing appropriate service delivery and therapeutic practice.
—*A. Toy Caldwell-Colbert, PhD, ABPP, Vice Chair for Psychological Services and Professor of Psychiatry, Department of Psychiatry, Howard University College of Medicine, Howard University Hospital, Washington, DC*

Psychotherapy is the most human of disciplines, so therapists must deal with their own humanity and its foibles if they are to be optimally helpful. Pope and colleagues successfully utilize the Socratic method to stimulate thought about feelings and help therapists feel better about their thoughts. They challenge common "myth-under-standings" about taboo topics and prescribe open self-examination and honest communication. This is a useful guide to often unexplored and dangerous territory.
—*David Spiegel, MD, Willson Professor and Associate Chair of Psychiatry and Behavioral Sciences, Stanford University School of Medicine, Stanford, CA; President, American College of Psychiatrists*

This fine book does not tell the reader what to do, but what to think about. It is one of those rare books that will be equally useful and valuable to graduate students and practicing professionals.
—*George Stricker, PhD, American School of Professional Psychology, Argosy University, Washington, DC*

More than a thought-provoking resource of useful reminders, valuable insights, and critical questions, this is a book that invites its readers to learn by doing and guides them through the experience. Those who take up the challenge will find themselves richly rewarded, both professionally and personally. I know that I was.
—*Douglas Saunders, PhD, President, Ontario Psychological Association; Assistant Professor, Faculty of Medicine, Department of Public Health Sciences, University of Toronto, Toronto, Ontario, Canada*

From the myths that need to be challenged, the taboos about therapists talking to consultants about the feelings that make them uncomfortable, and the embarrassing moments that are most challenging, Pope, Sonne, and Greene update the 1993 book with new scenarios to use as a guide. Every therapist who practices ethical interventions will want to learn the questions that are suggested to ask themselves about how to handle a whole range of difficult client issues including, of course, Pope's expert advice on what to do when sexual feelings are aroused in therapy. This book is MUST-reading and should be on every therapist's desk.

—*Lenore E. Walker, EdD, ABPP, Diplomate in Clinical and Family Psychology, Professor, Nova Southeastern University Center for Psychological Studies, Ft. Lauderdale, FL*

Pope, Sonne, and Greene have nicely outlined a host of issues that can arise in therapy but that trainees may be reluctant to bring up in supervision and more seasoned therapists may be reluctant to admit to their colleagues or even to themselves. They discuss reasons for our failure to discuss these issues, while noting their importance in rendering care for our patients and in taking care of ourselves, and they provide a framework to begin addressing the issues before they arise in therapy. The passages from historic documents and clinical scenarios for exploration and discussion should be of particular use in preparing for troublesome therapeutic situations.

—*David J. Martin, PhD, Chief Psychologist, Director of Training, Director, HIV Mental Health Services, Department of Psychiatry, Harbor-UCLA Medical Center, Torrance, CA*

This book challenges us to consider those most uncomfortable situations, as its question-focused vignettes ask us to deeply self-reflect on taboo topics. Dostoevsky, who opined that each person has ideas they hide even from him- or herself, would be proud of this tome's efforts to expose us to our own inner secrets and fears. A great thought piece for professionals of all experience levels.

—*Ed Lundeen, PhD, Private Practice, Allentown, PA; Editor,* Independent Practitioner

What Therapists Don't Talk About and Why should be required reading for both novice and expert clinicians. Drawing on the empirical literature and examples from clinical practice, this practical text challenges psychotherapists to consider issues that are often avoided and encourages honest reflection on the personal factors influencing the conduct of psychotherapy. It is a must-read for both novice and expert clinicians.

—*Edward Shafranske, PhD, ABPP, Professor and Director of the Doctoral Program in Clinical Psychology, Pepperdine University, Irvine, CA*

Pope, Sonne, and Greene are to be congratulated. With this new edition, the authors provide unthinkable conundrums, feelings elicited, and pathways to discuss and think through these previously untouchable areas. Their passages and scenarios—often therapist and trainees' worst fantasies—will provide rich substance for generations of therapists, faculty, and supervisors. This book will be indispensable for supervisors and practitioners alike. I can hardly wait to use it as a tool in supervision training.

—*Carol Falender, PhD, Independent Practice, Clinical Professor, Department of Psychology, University of California, Los Angeles*

This is one of those "wish I could have read it my first day in grad school" books. The topics this volume covers are the forbidden ones that every therapist struggles with; reading this book is like having a wise, compassionate, thoughtful teacher and consultant who gets you to think and feel, critically and deeply, about the strange human thing we call psychotherapy. I'll be recommending it to my students and colleagues.

—*Laura S. Brown, PhD, ABPP, Independent Practice, Seattle, WA*

When was the last time an excited colleague grabbed you by both shoulders and said, "I just read this wonderful book on ethics and psychotherapy"? Probably around the same time you last won the lottery. Often, reading about psychotherapy ethics is akin to reading the tax code—important, but statutory dry, and perhaps delivered with a hint of catechism-like castigation. *What Therapists Don't Talk About and Why* is different, in fact, unique. More than simply readable, it is entertaining, witty, and poignant. It is refreshingly accepting, human, and honest about the inner world of the psychotherapist. Rather than lay down a lockstep mode of ethical practice around specific issues, they walk the reader through a series of real-life vignettes, each time asking questions about the reader's reaction that induce discomfort and then help resolve it. The questioning method easily generalizes and, after a few repetitions, begins to form a new layer to one's ethical foundation. By the end of the book we emerge with a tried-and-true technique to apply to any ethical dilemma of psychotherapy; we are newly comfortable with the discomfort of the ethical bind. And we had a fun time getting there. What more can one ask?

—*Raymond E. Arsenault, PhD, Independent Practice, Andover, MA*

What a resource for teachers of ethics courses! . . . The book should be useful at all levels of training and experience.

—*Lynn P. Rehm, PhD, ABPP, Professor, Department of Psychology, University of Houston, Houston, TX*

Whatever the original or subsequent title of this book, it is essentially a superb text about the practice of psychotherapy, with all its unexpected twists, turns, and difficulties, for therapists and patients. From its excellent short courses on logical and ethical fallacies, to its astonishing variety of intensely provocative case examples with self-assessment questions, to its steamy discussions of therapists' sexual feelings, the book illuminates, in a nonthreatening, conversational tone, the previously avoided dimensions of the therapeutic endeavor. It belongs on the shelf of any therapist willing to learn or think critically about psychotherapy; it may also save one from a lot of frustration and heartbreak in the work.

—*Thomas G. Gutheil, MD, Professor of Psychiatry, Harvard Medical School, Boston, MA*

Endorsements for the 1993 Edition

Pope, Sonne, and Holroyd deserve kudos for having the courage to explore the unspoken. . . . Scholarly, engaging. . . the field of psychotherapy will never be the same again.

—*Donald Meichenbaum, Professor of Psychology, University of Waterloo, Waterloo, Ontario, Canada*

Required reading for all clinicians, interns, and other trainees.

—*A. T. Morales, DSW, Director of Clinical Social Work and Social Work Training, Department of Psychiatry and Biobehavioral Sciences, University of California, Los Angeles*

This superb new volume fills a void in the current literature. . . With a minimum of jargon and with clarity of prose style, the authors have provided a much-needed manual for psychotherapists of all theoretical orientations and all professional disciplines.

—*Glen Gabbard, MD, Vice President of Adult Services, The Menninger Clinic, Topeka, KS; Clinical Professor of Psychiatry, University of Kansas School of Medicine, Wichita; Training and Supervising Analyst, Topeka Institute for Psychoanalysis, Topeka, KS*

A landmark contribution. . . . There could be no more appropriate people to write this valuable resource.

—*Melba J. T. Vasquez, PhD, ABPP, Diplomate in Counseling Psychology; former Chair, Board for the Advancement of Psychology in the Public Interest, American Psychological Association*

Like a trusted confidant, this reassuring yet challenging book shows how research, theory, and the reader's own feelings can be used to guide clinical practice. It is that rarest of books with which the reader shares an intimate dialogue of personal discovery. Powerful, truthful, and adventurous, it will serve as an essential text to which seasoned therapists will return again and again and should be required reading in all training programs.

—*Jesse D. Geller, PhD, Department of Psychology, Yale University; Director, Yale Psychological Services Clinic, New Haven, CT*

What Therapists
Don't Talk About
and Why

What Therapists Don't Talk About and Why

UNDERSTANDING TABOOS THAT HURT US AND OUR CLIENTS

KENNETH S. POPE, JANET L. SONNE, AND BEVERLY GREENE

FOREWORDS BY
MELBA J. T. VASQUEZ AND
GERALD P. KOOCHER

American Psychological Association • Washington, DC

Fifth Printing November 2010

Published by
American Psychological Association
750 First Street, NE
Washington, DC 20002
www.apa.org

To order
APA Order Department
P.O. Box 92984
Washington, DC 20090-2984
Tel: (800) 374-2721; Direct: (202) 336-5510
Fax: (202) 336-5502; TDD/TTY: (202) 336-6123
Online: www.apa.org/books/
E-mail: order@apa.org

In the U.K., Europe, Africa, and the Middle East, copies may be ordered from
American Psychological Association
3 Henrietta Street
Covent Garden, London
WC2E 8LU England

Typeset in Palatino by Stephen D. McDougal, Mechanicsville, MD

Printer: Edwards Brothers, Inc., Ann Arbor, MI
Cover Designer: Naylor Design, Washington, DC
Technical/Production Editor: Devon Bourexis

The opinions and statements published are the responsibility of the authors, and such opinions and statements do not necessarily represent the policies of the American Psychological Association.

Library of Congress Cataloging-in-Publication Data

Pope, Kenneth S.
  What therapists don't talk about and why : understanding taboos that hurt us and our clients / Kenneth S. Pope, Janet L. Sonne, and Beverly Greene.
    p. cm.
  Includes bibliographical references and index.
  ISBN 1-59147-401-9—ISBN 1-59147-411-6 (hardcover)
    1. Psychotherapists. 2. Psychotherapist and patient. 3. Mythology. 4. Secrecy. I. Sonne, Janet L. II. Greene, Beverly. III. Title.
  [DNLM: 1. Psychotherapy—methods. 2. Psychotherapy—ethics. 3. Professional-Patient Relations. 4. Sexual Behavior—psychology. WM 420 P825w 2006]

RC480.5.P636 2006
616.89'14—dc22   2005028833

British Library Cataloguing-in-Publication Data
A CIP record is available from the British Library.

Printed in the United States of America
First Edition

Contents

About the Second Edition

The title of the 1993 first edition of this book was *Sexual Feelings in Psychotherapy: Explorations for Therapists and Therapists-in-Training*. The new title for the second edition—*What Therapists Don't Talk About and Why: Understanding Taboos That Hurt Us and Our Clients*—reflects a greatly expanded scope that focuses on a variety of other topics in addition to sexual feelings.

Foreword to the Second Edition: Things My Teachers Never Mentioned

Gerald P. Koocher

In his earlier book with Janet Sonne and Jean Holroyd (*Sexual Feelings in Psychotherapy: Explorations for Therapists and Therapists-in-Training*), Kenneth Pope took us into the challenging arena of topics that our teachers and supervisors in psychology and psychotherapy rarely, if ever, mentioned. This updated and expanded volume with Janet Sonne and Beverly Greene carries us into a broader range of challenging, but no less taboo, topics. Don't worry, sex is still covered, but so is the full range of issues that address the human nature of the psychotherapeutic enterprise. These include the basic myths of how one becomes and supposedly acts as a psychotherapist, what "real therapists" do or do not do behind closed doors, and the genuine struggles that occur daily as part of every psychotherapist's inner life.

I have heard it said that in the typical American family parents seldom talk openly about three topics: sex, death, and money. Psychotherapists are very willing to explore these topics with their clients, although they seldom reflect thoughtfully on how these same three issues influence daily decisions in their own lives and professional work. Is my time worth what I'm charging? How am I supposed to conduct myself when I feel bored, distracted, annoyed, or sexually aroused during a psychotherapy session? What should I do if therapy with a client seems stuck, adrift, or to be going in the wrong direction? Have I planned for the needs of my clients in the event that I become seriously disabled or die? What should I do when my personal values differ significantly from those of my patient? What should I do when I don't know what to do? Is it okay to be a "good enough" therapist, or must I pursue a mythical ideal of practice? Such topics comprise the soft underbelly of practice, seldom addressed during graduate school training in psychotherapy. These are sensitive, anxiety-provoking, often ignored, yet universal questions and concerns that we seldom feel comfortable discussing, even when we can find someone who might be willing to talk with us about them.

On occasion, I tell my students and professional audiences that I once spent an entire psychotherapy session holding hands with a 26-year-old woman together in a quiet darkened room. That disclosure usually elicits more than a few gasps and grimaces. When I add that I could not bring myself to end the session after 50 minutes and stayed with the young woman holding hands for another half hour, and when I add the fact that I never billed for the extra time, eyes roll. Then I explain that the young woman had cystic fibrosis with severe pulmonary disease and panic-inducing air hunger. She had to struggle through three breaths on an oxygen line before she could speak a sentence. I had come into her room, sat down by her bedside, and asked how I might help her. She grabbed my hand and said, "Don't let go." When the time came for another appointment, I called a nurse to take my place. By this point in my story, most listeners who had felt critical of or offended by the hand holding have moved from an assumption of sexualized impropriety to one of empathy and compassion. The real message of the anecdote, however, lies in the fact that I never learned this behavior in a classroom. No description of such an intervention exists in any treatment manual or tome on empirically based psychotherapy.

As a clinical supervisor I have learned to ask the therapists I work with about their own feelings in response to what transpires in their sessions. Sometimes they are candid, as when one told me with embarrassment that she became nauseous and had to flee a patient's room after viewing a postsurgical wound. Another told me of feeling both angry and helpless at his inability to stabilize a suicidal teenager with outpatient treatment. Yet another expressed great disappointment that she "became tearful and could not control" her feelings as she listened to a couple discuss the loss of their newborn to a congenital defect, as well as feeling guilty that she was at the time 2 months pregnant. At other times, my supervisees most likely will be less inclined to share feelings. They may fear I will give them a bad rating, refuse a letter of reference, or otherwise think less of them should they disclose that they experience feelings of intense anger, repulsion, or sexual attraction during the course of a therapy session.

In this era of privacy concerns in both health care and education, teachers and supervisors must walk a very fine line, striving to educate while not offending, invading privacy, or strongly challenging core values they may uncover in students and trainees. For example, Standard 7.04 (Student Disclosure of Personal Information) of the American Psychological Association's "Ethical Principles of Psychologists and Code of Conduct"[1] cautions that

> psychologists do not require students or supervisees to disclose personal information in course- or program-related activities, either orally or in writing, regarding sexual history, history of abuse and neglect, psychological treatment, and relationships with parents, peers, and spouses or significant others except if (1) the program or training facility has clearly identified this requirement in its admissions and program materials or (2) the information is necessary to evaluate or obtain assistance for students whose personal problems could reasonably be judged to be preventing them from performing their training- or professionally related activities in a competent manner or posing a threat to the students or others.

Effectively helping psychotherapists to deal with such sensitive issues may require addressing troubling past personal experiences. Pope and his colleagues effectively warn us about creating a climate in which such work can take place, while recognizing boundaries between personal and skill development as a psychotherapist and the need for personal psychotherapy. A respectful balance of exploration, respect, support, and introspection forms the foundation of optimal training in psychotherapy. Faculty, supervisors, and the graybeards among us must take on the challenge of helping our students, trainees, and junior colleagues get to that point. Pope and his colleagues have given us an excellent road map.

---

[1]American Psychological Association. (2002). Ethical principles of psychologists and code of conduct. *American Psychologist, 57*, 1060–1073; also available at http://www.apa.org/ethics/code2002.html

Apart from the strategy and tactics of psychotherapy, integrated with a knowledge of basic behavioral sciences, psychodiagnostic assessment, human development, and individual differences, we have historically done a poor job of teaching psychotherapists how to deal with our own intrapsychic human complexities. One possible exception is traditional psychoanalytic training, which generally demands contemporaneous treatment of selected clients and intensive personal psychotherapy focused on the treatment of the clients. This book provides substantial ammunition to begin that process as a kind of do-it-yourself guidebook and is much less expensive than psychoanalytic training.

Readers of this book, whether novices or advanced practitioners, will likely learn a great deal by reading and reflecting on the authors' ideas. I would recommend, however, reading it together with colleagues, teachers, and supervisors. Discussing the ideas with each other in a nondefensive, case-oriented manner will likely lead to considerably more learning for all involved. Such discussions will also pave the way for the more open types of collegial dialogue that significantly improve clinical practice and compensate for the things *our* teachers never mentioned.

Foreword to the 1993 Edition

Melba J. T. Vasquez

In the mental health professions, we have seen the number of ethical complaints continue to increase over the past decade, an increase driven in large part by therapists sexually exploiting their clients. As the research reviewed in Appendix C[1] suggests, as many as 10% of male therapists and 2% to 3% of female therapists have reported engaging in sex with current or former clients. Sex with clients continues to be a problem despite the fact that the prohibition against sex with clients has been the clearest and probably the most publicized explicit proscription in all ethics codes of the mental health professions.

Evidence exists that society feels that we have not done enough to monitor our own mental health professions. Because the professions have failed to address this problem adequately, the legal system has stepped in. Civil courts are awarding monetary damages to victims of sexual exploitation by therapists. Such exploitation is so damaging that it is being criminalized. As I write this foreword, sex with clients is already a felony in slightly over a half dozen[2] states, with offenders sometimes incurring stiff fines and prison terms of up to 10 years.

The outrage that many feel about this abuse and the professions' inadequate response to it was reflected in Ann Landers's[3] column "Not All Psychiatrists Are Bad; This One Was." Landers devoted her entire Sunday column to the book *You Must Be Dreaming*.[4] The book described how one of its authors, Barbara Noel,

---

This foreword is adapted from *Sexual Feelings in Psychotherapy: Explorations for Therapists and Therapists-in-Training* (pp. ix–xiii), by K. S. Pope, J. L. Sonne, and J. Holroyd, 1993, Washington, DC: American Psychological Association. Copyright 1993 by the American Psychological Association.

[1]This note refers to Appendix C of the 1993 edition.

[2]As of October 2005, 25 states had criminalized patient–therapist sex.

[3]Landers, A. (1992, October 11). Psychologist's [sic] abuse of patient strikes chord. *Austin American Statesman*, p. F2.

[4]Noel, B., & Watterson, K. (1992). *You must be dreaming*. New York: Poseidon.

was injected with Amytal, a barbiturate, and raped by psychiatrist Jules H. Masserman, a past president of the American Psychiatric Association and the American Academy of Psychoanalysis. Landers's rage was based in part on the perception that the psychiatric community protected Masserman by allowing him to relinquish quietly his license to practice and by declining to expel him from the American Psychiatric Association. At the time of her column, Masserman still sat on the American Psychiatric Association's Board of Trustees. Landers stated, "The psychiatric community does indeed take care of its own, but Ann Landers takes care of HER own, too, and this column will be read by 90 million people."[5] Approximately 1 month later, a letter from the current president of the American Psychiatric Association was published in an Ann Landers column mistitled by my local paper "Psychologist's [sic] Abuse of Patient Strikes Chord."[6] Joseph English applauded Landers's efforts to protect patients from exploitation, reiterated that doctor–patient sex is always wrong, acknowledged how important it is to publicize these violations more widely, and asserted that his association had taken action to do so.

This kind of public outcry can help our mental health professions to consider how we can begin to fulfill more adequately our responsibilities to restrict and prevent the damaging behavior of sex with clients. And that is why *Sexual Feelings in Psychotherapy: Explorations for Therapists and Therapists-in-Training* is a landmark contribution. It presents an opportunity for therapists and trainees to explore their reactions to sexual feelings to better understand assumptions, behaviors, and approaches to clients and to the process of counseling and psychotherapy.

Most of us do not have sex with our clients. However, in our practice, we are presented with an almost infinite number of situations and circumstances in which we have the power to exploit, abuse, and hurt our clients. The unique approach presented in this book allows us to sensitize ourselves to many ethical and therapeutic issues. Most important, it provides us with the opportunity to improve our ability to reason about sexual issues.

---

[5]See footnote 3, this foreword.

[6]Landers, A. (1992, September 13). Not all psychiatrists are bad; this one was. *Austin American Statesman*, p. E2.

The book does so in part by presenting a variety of scenarios and passages that can be discussed with others regarding optimal ways of handling the situations. The passages and scenarios are meant to call the reader's attention to situations, behaviors, or feelings that may seem taboo and that tend to make many professionals and professionals-in-training uncomfortable. The book encourages acknowledgment and exploration of feelings and reactions elicited by the passages and scenarios as well as by the clinical situations we encounter daily.

Several important assumptions of the authors warrant special emphasis. One is that most therapists have experienced sexual attraction to clients and that this attraction tends to make therapists uncomfortable. Although these attractions and subsequent discomfort are common, the therapist often feels alone in this experience. Therefore, much of the process of exploration and discovery of the therapist's feelings and reactions is best done in the company of others. The process of open discussion of feelings and reactions can help us to emerge from discomfort, shame, and guilt and to move toward ethically and clinically sound problem solving. It is crucial to find appropriate ways to acknowledge and accept sexual feelings in therapy and the complex cognitive, affective, and physical responses to these feelings.

A major theme of the book is that there is no lockstep process or absolute formula for handling such situations. The issues raised are intended to provide an opportunity for self-exploration and discovery. There are no absolutes for how to handle uncomfortable situations that arise in the therapeutic situation, save the most fundamental rule: The authors emphasize that under no circumstances should a therapist ever have sex with a client, and under no circumstances should a therapist ever communicate, either explicitly or implicitly, that sexual intimacies with a client are a possibility. It is solely the therapist's responsibility to ensure that no sexual intimacies occur with a patient. Yet there are no clear or easy answers as to what to do if one experiences sexual feelings for a patient. No "cookbook" approach exists to guide the therapist. Yet one can go through the helpful process of clarifying values, styles, and preferences in managing responses. One chapter of this book, for example, offers valuable insights into the contextual factors that may influence therapists' sexual feelings and responses, including religion, sexual orientation, gender, age, ethnicity, social class, disability, client diagnosis, client physical attractiveness, and therapist orientation. And the appendixes, as another example, offer several articles that provide important research findings about therapist–client sexual issues.

Readers of this text are encouraged to avoid judging behaviors described in the passages and scenarios as right or wrong, sound or unsound, appropriate or inappropriate, but to attend to their own unique cognitive and emotional reactions. This approach fosters readers' emotional learning and professional development. For experienced therapists, the passages and scenarios will indeed stir memories of situations in which they have found themselves and provide opportunities to reflect on what they did at the time and what they might do differently now. For therapists-in-training, the passages and scenarios provide vivid images from the wide range of situations in which they will inevitably find themselves during the course of a career.

This book is a contribution that is long overdue. Training programs are often at a loss as to how to foster therapists' sense of responsibility for ethical behavior in their relationships with clients. One of the key strategies in the prevention of therapist–client sexual contact is trainees' understanding of the many issues raised in this book. The passages and scenarios will evoke and serve as the focus of rich and valuable discussions that will promote self-awareness and knowledge in such areas as attraction to clients, the role of touch in therapy, vulnerabilities, boundaries and so many other vital aspects of counseling and therapy. Knowledge and understanding that come as a result of these discussions can help sensitize trainees to the potential impact of their behavior with clients. They can help lead, for example, to increased awareness of how therapists may at times unwittingly sexualize relationships with clients.

Few of us in the mental health professions take our work lightly, and most of us are highly motivated to behave ethically in all of our work. When we do commit ethical errors, we often do so out of ignorance, and from not ever having been exposed to the complex and difficult situations in which we find ourselves. This resource is a tremendous contribution to increasing skills in managing the tremendous anxiety and uncertainty about our decisions and behaviors that affect so deeply the lives of our clients. We have an ethical responsibility to develop the abilities to monitor ourselves, our colleagues, and our profession. This book will go far in providing a means to promote those abilities.

The authors are distinguished and outstanding psychologists with international reputations for their rigorous innovative work in the area of ethics and clinical standards of practice and especially for their pioneering, landmark contributions to our understanding of sexual issues in counseling and psychotherapy. Kenneth S. Pope, Janet L. Sonne, and Jean C. Holroyd have all dedicated much time and energy to the promotion of professionals' responsibility in their behavior with clients. All have served on ethics committees or task forces to develop codes and standards for psychologists. There could be no more appropriate people to write this valuable resource.

What Therapists
Don't Talk About
and Why

1

Questioning Myths, Taboos, Secrets, and Uncomfortable Topics

Our education takes shape not just from what's in textbooks, graduate programs, and internships but from what's missing—what we don't see, acknowledge, or talk about. The relative silence about so many of the topics in this book is part of our education. We learn what topics are to be ignored, treated as secrets, denied, discounted, or examined no longer than you would hold a hot potato.

We go to our careers unprepared to address these topics realistically. We learn the processes of avoidance, masking, and minimization and begin to model them for our colleagues, our clients, our students, and the public.

This is a book of exploration, discovery, and learning. It was created to help therapists and therapists-in-training explore topics that are taboo, that receive only superficial treatment, or that provoke anxiety, discomfort, and confusion. They put us at risk in some way. We can avoid, mask, or minimize them so effectively that they become invisible to us.

The 1993 edition of this book focused on taboos around therapists' sexual feelings, arousal, and fantasies. This second edition explores a wider range of topics, including feelings of incompetence; therapists' blunders; fee disasters; hatred for a patient; therapists getting sick, growing old, and dying; confusion about disability and accessibility; prayer with patients as part of therapy; boredom; patients with terrible body odor; therapists' fears and

3

terrors; sexual orientation and self-disclosure; vulnerability; therapists' shame and guilt; silence about research data that are influential but faked; difficult aspects of race and ethnicity; anger at patients; the experience of being fired; confusion about what to do; and betrayal of ourselves, our profession, and our values to get ahead or just survive.

Like the original 1993 book, this new edition avoids imposing "right" answers and clinging to traditional, "politically correct," "emotionally correct," or "psychologically correct" approaches. As described later, the book's model of learning encourages a mindful awareness of the complex, messy situations that occur in real life, of how we respond to them, and of the need for openness, honesty, courage, and constant questioning. The book has been created for use by individual therapists or in courses, workshops, peer-consultation, or study groups (please see chap. 3).

Basic Myths About the Psychotherapist

Why is it so easy to avoid these topics and so hard to talk about them openly, honestly, and realistically? Part of the answer may lie in the myths we have constructed about psychotherapists.

Where do these myths come from, and why do we live by them? There are as many reasons as there are myths. It's tempting to create an idealized version of ourselves to hide our flaws, mistakes, and vulnerabilities. Some clients hold flattering images of us, and we take the bait. Clinging to myths can make us feel safe when the world or our work scares us or makes us feel insecure. Myths comfort us when what happens in therapy makes us feel sad, frustrated, enraged, aroused, or hopeless. Most myths look like time-savers: If money will take care of itself, for example, there's no reason to waste time studying business principles, discussing how to set fees, or learning how to market a practice.[1]

The myths map out taboo areas and turn us away from them. If, for example, a myth denies therapists' sexuality or competi-

---

[1]See chapters 2, 7, and 9 of Pope, K. S., & Vasquez, M. J. T. (2005). *How to survive and thrive as a therapist: Information, ideas, and resources for psychologists in practice*. Washington, DC: American Psychological Association.

tiveness, it can produce the emperor's new clothes in reverse: We don't see them when they're there. Or if we see them, we keep quiet about them.

Do we actually believe these myths? Hard to say. Most make us laugh if we give them a moment's thought. But we act as if we believe them. We set up training curricula, guide classroom discussions, provide resources, plan careers, and evaluate our progress as if the myths were true.

Although it is likely that all of us have been vulnerable to at least some of these myths, they represent unrealistic thinking about who we are as psychotherapists. As we recognize and come to terms with these errors in thinking about psychotherapists, we prepare ourselves to talk more frankly about topics that tend to be taboo. Part of this book's purpose is to provide tools—see particularly chapters 5 and 7—that will be helpful in identifying myths and taboos and avoiding rationalizations, fallacies, and evasions in examining them and their implications.

Here are just a few of the myths that afflict our training and practice. It is almost certain that every reader of this book could extend this list, and we encourage classes, workshops, and study groups not only to question whether the myths listed here have influenced their own settings but to identify influential myths that don't appear here.

MYTH: Therapists learn therapy and practice in organizations free of competition's influence.

OK, you can stop laughing now. No, really, you'll get the hiccups. It seems strange that a myth could flourish that is so at odds with reality. The system of grading puts us in competition with each other from our earliest years. Grading on the curve intensifies the process: A grade of 60% might be excellent or failing, depending on how well the other students did on the test. Many of us remember being asked, at the end of a test, to pledge in writing that "I have neither given nor received help on this test." We compete—with our grades, GRE scores, letters of recommendation, interviews, and other criteria—for admission to graduate school. Once in graduate school, we continue to compete—for grades, for teaching and research assistantships, for letters of recommendation, for internships, and so on, as well as for the intangibles, such as "to be the most [insert desired quality—such as intelligent, well-prepared, wise, competent, articulate, likable—here] student in the class." We learn from professors who are also competing—for tenure, office space, grant money, promotions, raises, and, at least sometimes, attention, prestige, and popularity. This competition can lead to interesting behavior. In more than one graduate program, a reference book put on reserve before an exam, so that every student can check it out only for an hour, has gone mysteriously missing. Students may start circulating rumors about their competitors, rumors that are creative, plausible sounding, reputation destroying, and false.

The degree to which we are competing in so many ways with each other in a system that fosters competition provides a context in which opening up, failing to mask our weaknesses, allowing ourselves to be vulnerable, speaking frankly, acknowledging our mistakes (especially when no one else has discovered them), and engaging in genuine exploration and discovery may be a handicap, ready for skillful exploitation by those who see taking down others as a way for them to advance in the competition.

Some of the greatest difficulties seem to occur when the history, context, and process of competition are not acknowledged, when everyone acts as if learning and practicing therapy occur in settings free of competition's influence. This can make people feel a little crazy, everyone assuming that only he or she feels that way. It can isolate people and throw them off stride. It can make people mistrust their own feelings, perception, and judgment.

This myth is *not* about whether competition per se is helpful, hurtful, mixed, or "it depends." It is about the degree to which the presence and influence of competition may have become invisible, unacknowledged, unexamined, and unspoken.

MYTH: If you're a good therapist, the money will take care of itself.

The effects of this myth can be seen in the number of therapists who finish their graduate training without any education in fundamental business principles. So many of us know nothing of how to construct a realistic and effective business plan, how to budget for an office and other expenses, how to market our practice, or how to anticipate the financial seasons of a practice.

The myth also makes itself felt in the relative lack of attention that many graduate programs pay to therapy fees. It is as if there were a belief that fee setting, fee collection, what to do about late payments, what to do about people who refuse to pay their bills, and so on were either irrelevant to the therapy or so easy that we therapists need little or no training in that area.

The difficulty acknowledging the role that fees can play both in the therapy itself and in the therapist's attempts to make a living has deep historical roots. Large volumes that reviewed psychotherapy research tended to ignore the topic completely, prompting one author to comment,

> As a footnote, I would like to remark that if a Martian read the volumes reporting the two psychotherapy conferences and if he read all the papers of this conference it would never occur to him that psychotherapy is something done for money. Either therapists believe money is not a worthwhile research variable or money is part of the new obscenity in which we talk more freely about sex but never mention money. (p. 539)[2]

Nobett Mintz[3] once termed fees a "tabooed subject," suggesting that various factors "functioned to inhibit therapists from inquiring too closely into the financial side of psychotherapeutic practice and the actual effects it may have on the therapeutic enterprise" (p. 37). Tom Gutheil[4] noted that little had changed in this regard in his 1986 chapter in Krueger's book, *The Last Taboo: Money as Symbol and Reality in Psychotherapy and Psychoanalysis*.

MYTH: Therapists are invulnerable, immortal, and ageless.

A colleague of one of the authors had worked for years at a hospital and community mental health center. One day, a docile

---

[2]Colby, K. (1968). Commentary: Report to plenary session on psychopharmacology in relation to psychotherapy. In J. M. Schlein (Ed.), *Research in psychotherapy* (Vol. 3, pp. 536–540). Washington, DC: American Psychological Association.

[3]Mintz, N. L. (1971). Patient fees and psychotherapeutic transactions. *Journal of Consulting and Clinical Psychology, 36*, 1–8.

[4]Gutheil, T. C. (1986). Fees in beginning private practice. In D. Krueger (Ed.), *The last taboo: Money as symbol and reality in psychotherapy and psychoanalysis* (pp. 175–188). London: Brunner-Routledge.

and somewhat confused day-treatment patient asked for directions to the office of someone who would be conducting a psychological assessment. The colleague, who was headed toward that wing of the center, offered to escort the patient to the office.

As they walked down one of the corridors, the patient pulled a knife, forced the colleague into a deserted room, and, locking the door behind them, held her hostage. The patient began to hallucinate and threatened to kill her. Although the center's staff noticed the therapist was not showing up for her appointments, no one knew where she was. Hours later, she was able to talk the patient into giving up his knife and letting her go.

In the weeks and months after this harrowing experience, the therapist tried to understand why she had ignored the warning signs that became clear in retrospect and had made herself vulnerable to such risks with no backup plans about how to handle them. In part, she thought, it was because she'd come to feel safe in "her" center and ignored risks and warnings that she'd be alert to if she were walking down the street or even visiting in another facility. Feeling safe and secure—although this feeling reflected a myth—in her familiar work setting had become an unexamined part of her identity.

The myth of the invulnerable, immortal, ageless therapist is reflected in the number of therapists who complete their training without learning how to set up a practice office with an eye toward safety—how to screen new clients, what to do if a client pulls a weapon during a session, how to secure a therapy office and waiting room in light of potential violence, what arrangements to make to summon help in the event of violence or the immediate threat of violence, and so on.

The myth is reflected also in the number of therapists who practice without an adequate professional will and other arrangements. It is difficult to acknowledge in a real and practical way that any of us could at any moment experience a stroke, a heart attack, an accident, a criminal attack requiring hospitalization, or any of the other diverse illnesses, disorders, incidents, and misfortunes that can prevent us—temporarily or permanently—from functioning as therapists.

Imagine the consequences when a therapist in individual or group practice suddenly dies without having made a professional will.[5] Colleagues may not only be coping with their shock and grief over their sudden loss of a friend but also be forced to scramble to find the keys to their friend's therapy office and filing cabinets, the passwords to their Palm Pilot and computer, where schedules and contact information are stored, the code to retrieve answering machine messages, and so on; during which the friend's clients—some of them in crisis—are showing up at the office for their appointments and leaving messages, some of them urgent, on the friend's answering machine.

The myth's influence can be seen also in the number of therapists who continue to practice when Alzheimer's disease or other age-related factors have impaired their ability to function adequately as a therapist.[6] We tend to avoid planning for the contingencies of aging. We don't want to monitor ourselves and ask trusted colleagues to attend to any signs that we are losing our competence.

MYTH: With their extensive education and training, therapists have a firm grasp of logic and, whatever the limits of their knowledge, do not fall prey to basic logical fallacies.

Courses in the various forms of logical reasoning seem relatively rare in graduate psychology programs, continuing education programs, and workshops. The myth seems to assume either that psychologists have an inherent grasp of logical thinking or that we somehow pick it up along the way.

Few myths grant us as much power as this one. Faced with a devastating critique of our own pet hypothesis, one that brings empirical data and sound reasoning to show that our falsifiable hypothesis is in fact false, we can easily dismiss the critique with an argumentum ad logicam, argumentum ad ignorantiam, or straw person argument. Or we could dismiss the person who wrote the critique with an ad hominem attack or *tu quoque* response.

---

[5]Pope, K. S., & Vasquez, M. J. T. (2005). *How to survive and thrive as a therapist: Information, ideas, and resources for psychologists in practice.* Washington, DC: American Psychological Association.

[6]Pope, K. S., & Vasquez, M. J. T. (1998). *Ethics in psychotherapy and counseling: A practical guide,* (2nd ed.). San Francisco: Jossey-Bass.

Lapses in logic unfortunately find their way into classroom discussions, peer-reviewed journal articles, and especially the polarized debates of controversial topics. Because logically flawed statements can sound so convincing—at least when used to support something that we ourselves value, believe in, or hope for—they blend in and are easy to miss. They have worked their way into so many forms of our discourse that it is worth pausing here to look at some of the most common forms of errors in reasoning. Here are some logical missteps that can trip up most of us at one time or another.[7]

Ad Hominem

The *argumentum ad hominem*, or *ad feminam*, attempts to discredit an argument or position by drawing attention to characteristics of the person who is making the argument or who holds the position.

Example: "The research and reasoning that supposedly support (or that supposedly discredit) this intervention are a joke. The researchers are people who are not methodologically sophisticated, and there have been rumors—I have no idea whether they're true or not—that they faked some of the data. The advocates (or opponents) of this intervention are the worst kind of sloppy thinkers. They are fanatical adherents who already have their minds made up; they've become true believers in their cause. They make arguments only a stupid person would accept, and mistakes in reasoning that would make an undergrad psychology major blush. These are not the kind of people who deserve to be taken seriously."

Affirming the Consequent

This fallacy takes the form of

If x, then y.

y.

Therefore, x.

Example: "People who are psychotic act in a bizarre manner. This person acts in a bizarre manner. Therefore, this person is psychotic."

---

[7]This section is adapted from "Falacies and Pitfalls in Psychology" © Ken Pope, available at http://kspope.com.

Alternate example: "If this client is competent to stand trial, she will certainly know the answers to at least 80% of the questions on this standardized test. She knows the answers to 87% of the test questions. Therefore, she is competent to stand trial."

Appeal to Ignorance (Ad Ignorantium)

The *appeal to ignorance* fallacy takes this form:

> There is no (or insufficient) evidence establishing that x is false.
> Therefore, x is true.

Example: "In the 6 years that I have been practicing my new and improved brand of cognitive–humanistic–dynamic–behavioral–decontructive–metaregressive–deontological psychotherapy (now with biofeedback!), which I developed, there has not been one published study showing that it fails to work or that it has ever harmed a patient. It is clearly one of the safest and most effective interventions ever devised."

Argument to Logic (Argumentum ad Logicam)

The *argument to logic* fallacy takes the form of assuming that a proposition must be false because an argument offered in support of that proposition was fallacious.

Example: "This new test seemed so promising, but the three studies that supported its validity turned out to have critical methodological flaws, so the test is probably not valid."

Begging the Question (Petitio Principii)

This fallacy, one of the fallacies of circularity, takes the form of arguments or other statements that simply assume or restate their own truth rather than providing relevant evidence and logical arguments.

Examples: Sometimes this fallacy literally takes the form of a question, such as, "Has your psychology department stopped teaching that ineffective approach to therapy yet?" (The question assumes—and a "yes" or "no" response to the question affirms—that the approach is ineffective.) Or, "Why must you always take positions that are so unscientific?" (The question assumes that all of the person's positions are unscientific.) Sometimes this fallacy takes the form of a statement such as, "No one can deny that [my theoretical orientation] is the only valid theoretical orientation" or "It must be acknowledged that [whatever psychological test battery I use] is the only legitimate test battery." Sometimes it takes the form of a logical argument, such as, "My new method of conducting meta-analyses is the most valid there is because it is the only one capable of such validity, the only one that has ever approached such validity, and the only one that is so completely valid."

Composition Fallacy

This fallacy takes the form of assuming that a group possesses the characteristics of its individual members.

Example: "Several years ago, a group of 10 psychologists started a psychology training program. Each of those psychologists is efficient, effective, and highly regarded. Their training program must be efficient, effective, and highly regarded."

Denying the Antecedent

This fallacy takes the form of

If x, then y.
Not x.
Therefore, not y.

Example: "If this test were based on fraudulent norms, then it would be invalid. But the norms are not fraudulent. Therefore, this test is valid."

Disjunctive Fallacy

This fallacy takes the form of

Either x or y.
x.
Therefore, not y.

Example: "These test results are clearly wrong, and it must be either because the client was malingering or because I bungled the test administration. Taking another look at the test manual, I see now that I bungled the test administration. Therefore, the client was not malingering."

Division Fallacy

The division fallacy or decomposition fallacy takes the form of assuming that the members of a group posses the characteristics of the group.

Example: "This clinic sure makes a lot of money. Each of the psychologists who work there must earn a large income."

False Analogy

The *false*, or *faulty*, *analogy* fallacy takes the form of argument by analogy in which the comparison is misleading in at least one important aspect.

Example: "There were wonderful psychologists who passed away several decades ago. If they could be effective in what they did without reading any of the studies or other articles that have been published in the last several decades, there's no need for me to read any of those works to be effective."

False Dilemma

Also known as the *either–or* fallacy or the fallacy of *false choices*, this fallacy takes the form of only acknowledging two (one of which is usually extreme) options from a continuum or other array of possibilities.

Example: "Either we accept the findings of this study demonstrating that this new intervention is the best to be used for this disorder, or we must no longer call ourselves scientists, psychologists, or reasonable people."

Golden Mean Fallacy

The fallacy of the *golden mean* (or fallacy of *compromise*, or fallacy of *moderation*) takes the form of assuming that the most valid conclusion is that which accepts the best compromise between two competing positions.

Example: "In our psychology department, half of the faculty believes that a behavioral approach is the only valid approach; the other half believes that the only valid approach is psychodynamic. Obviously, the most valid approach must be one that incorporates both behavioral and psychodynamic elements."

Mistaking Deductive Validity for Truth

This fallacy takes the form of assuming that because an argument is a logical syllogism, the conclusion must be true. It ignores the possibility that the premises of the argument may be false.

Example: "I just read a book proving that book's author can do much better than any psychological test at determining whether someone is malingering. The book's author reviews the literature showing that no psychological test is perfect at identifying malingering. All have at least some false positives and false negatives. But the author has a new method of identifying malingerers. All he does is listen to the sound of their voices as they say a sentence or two. And he included in the book a chart showing that by using this method, he has never been wrong in hundreds of cases. This proves his method is better than using psychological tests."

Naturalistic Fallacy

The *naturalistic* fallacy takes the form of logically deducing values (e.g., what is good, best, right, ethical, or moral) based only on statements of fact.

Example: "There is no intervention for victims of domestic violence that has more empirical support from controlled studies than this one. It is clear that this is the right way to address this problem, and we should all be providing this therapy whenever victims of domestic violence come to us for help."

Post Hoc, Ergo Propter Hoc (After This, Therefore on Account of This)

The *post hoc, ergo propter hoc* fallacy takes the form of confusing correlation with causation and concluding that because *y* follows *x*, then *y* must be a result of *x*.

Example: "My new sport psychology intervention works! I chose the player with the lowest batting average based on the last game from each of the teams in our amateur baseball league. Then I gave each of them my 5-minute intervention. And almost all of them improved their batting average in the next game!" (Note: This example may also involve the statistical phenomenon of regression to the mean.)

Red Herring

This fallacy takes the form of introducing or focusing on irrelevant information to distract from the valid evidence and reasoning. It takes its name from the strategy of dragging a herring across the path to distract hounds and other tracking dogs and to throw them off the scent of whatever they were searching for.

Example: "Some of you have objected to the new test batteries that were purchased for our program, alleging that they have no demonstrable validity, were not adequately normed for the kind of clients we see, and are unusable for clients who are physically disabled. What you have conveniently failed to mention, however, is that they cost less than a third of the price, are much easier to learn, and can be administered and scored in less than half the time compared with the tests we used to use."

Straw Person

The *straw person*, or *straw man*, or *straw woman* fallacy takes the form of mischaracterizing someone else's position in a way that makes it weaker, false, or ridiculous.

Example: "Those who believe in behavior modification obviously want to try to control everyone by subjecting them to rewards and punishments."

Tu Quoque (You Too!)

This fallacy takes the form of distracting attention from error or weakness by claiming that an opposing argument, person, or position has the same error or weakness.

Example: "I have been accused of using an ad hominem approach in trying to defend my research. But those who attack me and my research are also using ad hominem. And they started it!"

MYTH: Learning ethical standards, principles, and guidelines, along with examples of how they have been applied, translates into ethical practice.

It is difficult for many of us to let go of this myth. When the subject is ethics, so many licensing exams, graduate courses, and workshops focus almost exclusively on knowledge of formal ethics codes, their history and evolution, their relation to legal standards, and figuring out which code sections might be applicable to specific situations.

It is as if the answers to our ethical questions were already there in the code, waiting to tell us what to do, if only we were sufficiently familiar with it and could open ourselves up completely to it and listen intently and passively receive its wisdom without static or interference. However, what the code says is the beginning, not the end, of ethical consideration, of an ethical response to a situation.[8,9]

It is important not only to understand the nature and complexity of the considerations that are informed, but not determined, by the code but also to become aware of and appreciate the subtle ways in which all of us are vulnerable to cognitive strategies that allow us to evade ethical responsibilities while protesting, sometimes a little too loudly, that we are upholding the highest ethics and that anyone who disagrees or questions our reasoning is wrong, stupid, naive, and probably an all-around bad person. We may become indignant and accuse these others of be-

---

[8]See footnote 6, this chapter.
[9]Please see chapter 7, section entitled "The Legal and Ethical Framework."

ing unethical and of refusing to acknowledge our virtue and righteousness.

These cognitive strategies may rely on subtle rationalizations, appealing fallacies, doublespeak, or Alice-in-Wonderland maneuvers to make even the most selfish, thoughtless, harmful, or inhumane behavior come across as ethically ideal. Our awareness of the ways that each of us as individuals may be vulnerable— particularly at times of stress or fatigue, of great temptation or temporary weakness—to these cognitive strategies may be an important aspect of our ability to respond ethically to difficult and complex situations, particularly at moments when we are not at our best. Our ability to recognize these maneuvers as we are falling prey to them and to avoid, however reluctantly, their seeming rewards may be as influential to an ethical response as a knowledge of the ethics code.

What sorts of cognitive strategies are commonly used to justify unethical behavior as ethical? Here are a few. We encourage readers to expand the list.

1. It's not unethical as long as a managed care administrator or insurance case reviewer required or suggested it.
2. It's not unethical if we can use the passive voice and look ahead. If it is discovered that our CV is full of degrees we never earned, positions we never held, and awards we never received, all we need do is nondefensively acknowledge that mistakes were made and it's time to move on.
3. It's not unethical if we're victims. If we need to justify our victim status, we can always use one of two traditional scapegoats: (a) our "anything-goes" society, lacking any clear standards, that lets what were once solid rules drift and leaves us all ethically adrift or, conversely, (b) our coercive, intolerant society, tyrannized by "political correctness," that is always dumbing us down and keeping us down. Imagine, for example, we are arrested for speeding while drunk, and the person whose car we hit decides vengefully to press charges. We can show ourselves as the real victim by writing books and appearing on television pointing out that the legal system has been hijacked by a vicious minority of politically correct, self-serving tyrants who refuse to acknowledge that most speeding while

drunk is not only harmless but constructive, getting driv-
ers to their destinations faster and in better spirits. Those
who question our claims and reasoning are clearly intolerant, trying to silence us and destroy our right to do what is
right.

4. It's not unethical as long as we can name others who do
the same thing.

5. It's not unethical as long as there is no body of universally
accepted, methodologically perfect (i.e., without any flaws,
weaknesses, or limitations) studies showing—without any
doubt whatsoever—that exactly what we did was the necessary and sufficient proximate cause of harm to the client
and that the client would otherwise be free of all physical
and psychological problems, difficulties, or challenges. This
view was succinctly stated by a member of the Texas pes-
ticide regulatory board charged with protecting Texas citi-
zens against undue risks from pesticides. In discussing
chlordane, a chemical used to kill termites, one member
said, "Sure, it's going to kill a lot of people, but they may
be dying of something else anyway" (p. 17).[10]

6. It's not unethical if we acknowledge the importance of
judgment, consistency, and context. For example, it may
seem as if a therapist who has submitted hundreds of thou-
sands of dollars worth of bogus insurance claims for patients he never saw might have behaved "unethically."
However, as attorneys and others representing such professionals often point out: It was simply an error in judgment, completely inconsistent with the high ethics mani-
fest in every other part of the person's life, and insignificant
in the context of the unbelievable good that this person
does.

7. It's not unethical as long as no law was broken.

8. It's not unethical if we can say any of the following about
it (feel free to extend the list):
"What else could I do?"
"Anyone else would've done the same thing."
"It came from the heart."
"I listened to my soul."
"I went with my gut."
"It was the smart thing to do."

---

[10]Perspectives. (1990, April 23). *Newsweek*, p. 17.

"It was just common sense."
"I just knew that's what the client needed."
"I'd do the same thing again if I had it to do over."
"It worked before."
"I'm only human, you know!"
"What's the big deal?"

9. It's not unethical if the American Psychological Association, the American Psychiatric Association, the American Counseling Association, the National Association of Social Workers, or a similar organization allows it.
10. It's not unethical as long as we didn't mean to hurt anyone.
11. It's not unethical even if our acts have caused harm as long as the person harmed has failed to behave perfectly, is in some way unlikable, or is acting unreasonably.
12. It's not unethical if we have written an article, chapter, or book about it.
13. It's not unethical as long as we were under a lot of stress. No fair-minded person would hold us accountable for what we did when it is clear that it was the stress we were under—along with all sorts of other powerful factors—that must be held responsible.
14. It's not unethical as long as no one ever complained about it.
15. It's not unethical as long as our clients' condition (probably borderline) made them so difficult to treat and so troublesome and risky to be around that they elicited whatever it was we did (not, of course, to admit that we actually did anything).
16. It's not unethical as long as we don't talk about ethics. The principle of general denial is at work here. As long as no one mentions ethical aspects of practice, no course of action could be identified as unethical.
17. It's not unethical as long as we don't know a law, ethical principle, or professional standard that prohibits it. This rationalization encompasses two principles: specific ignorance and specific literalization. The principle of specific ignorance states that even if there is, say, a law prohibiting an action, what we do is not illegal as long as we don't know about the law. The principle of literalization states that if we cannot find specific mention of a particular incident anywhere in legal, ethical, or professional standards,

it must be ethical. In desperate times, when the specific incident is unfortunately mentioned in the standards and we are aware of it, it is still perfectly ethical as long as the standard does not mention our theoretical orientation. Thus, if the formal standard prohibits sexual involvement with patients, violations of confidentiality, or diagnosing without actually meeting with the client, a behavioral, humanistic, or psychodynamic therapist may legitimately engage in these activities as long as the standard does not explicitly mention behavioral, humanistic, or psychodynamic therapy.

18. It's not unethical as long as there are books, articles, or papers claiming that it is the right thing to do.

19. It's not unethical as long as a friend of ours knew someone who said an ethics committee somewhere once issued an opinion that it's OK.

20. It's not unethical as long as we know that legal, ethical, and professional standards were made up by people who don't understand the hard realities of psychological practice.

21. It's not unethical as long as we know that the people involved in enforcing standards (e.g., licensing boards or administrative law judges) are dishonest, stupid, destructive, and extremist; are unlike us in some significant way; or are conspiring against us.

22. It's not unethical as long as it results in a higher income or more prestige (i.e., is necessary).

23. It's not unethical as long as it would be really hard to do things another way.

24. It's not unethical as long as no one else finds out—or if whoever might find out probably wouldn't care anyway.

25. It's not unethical if we could not (or did not) anticipate the unintended consequences of our acts.

26. It's not unethical as long as we can find a consultant who says it's OK.

27. It's not unethical as long as the client asked us to do it.

28. It's not unethical as long as we don't intend to do it more than once.

29. It's not unethical as long as we're very important and can consider ourselves beyond ethics. The criteria for importance in this context generally include being rich, well known, extensively published, or tenured; having a large

practice; having what we think of as a "following" of likeminded people; or having discovered and given clever names to at least five new diagnoses described on television talk shows as reaching epidemic proportions. Actually, if we just think we're important, we'll have no problem finding proof.

30. It's not unethical as long as we're busy. After all, given our workload and responsibilities, who could reasonably expect us to obtain informed consent from all our clients, keep our chart notes in a secured area, be thorough when conducting assessments, and follow every little law?

The Nature and Reality of Myths, Taboos, Secrets, and Uncomfortable Topics

What do these myths suggest about the implicit image of the therapist we try to live up to or grow into, plan our training and practice around, and measure ourselves against?

One possible response to that question is that this image represents an invalid, unrealistic, and downright wrong standard for us, our development, and our work. We seem to be trying to hold ourselves to a standard requiring us to be immortal, invulnerable, ageless therapists, unaffected by competition, to whom the principles of business, finance, and logic come so naturally that we need no formal training in them and for whom ethical behavior is mainly a matter of knowing the ethics code and examples of how to apply it.

The purpose of this short book is to invite exploration and discussion of such myths; the taboos, secrets, and uncomfortable topics they foster; the errors in thinking they represent; and their implications for our development and work. As will become apparent in the following pages, this book's model of exploration, discovery, and learning depends in part on the reader's ability and readiness to be relentlessly honest about topics, experiences, and responses that most of us find it difficult to acknowledge. The process invites us to go beyond stances, views, and words that are safe and familiar, that are socially acceptable, that seem clearly right or at least clear. It is relatively easy for many of us to speak, endorse, or accept that which some view as "politically incorrect" or what turns out to be "a minority of one"; it is much harder for us to give voice to that which is "emotionally incorrect" or "psychologically incorrect."

The process also calls for us to reflect on and discuss our own experience, which will likely have both unique and shared aspects with the experiences of others. Those sharing the same setting at the same time can have sharply divergent experiences.

In the following passage, Beverly Greene reflects on topics that seemed unapproachable at the time—the late 1970s and early 1980s—although some or all have since become mainstream in some settings, are treated in glancing and incomplete ways in others, and remain almost untouchable in still others.

> When I think back on my own graduate and practicum training there were a lot of topics that either were not discussed or elicited enormous anxiety when they were raised. At that time perhaps the most anxiety provoking was race and racism. Generally there was a reluctance among faculty to acknowledge the impact of race and racism on not only the development and conduct of African American clients but also the therapeutic relationship itself.
>
> Usually such issues were raised exclusively by Black students much to what appeared to be the impatience and the consternation of both White students and faculty. It often seemed that students who raised these issues related to therapy or psychological testing or for that matter the somewhat racist history of psychology itself,[11] were viewed as though they were hypersensitive, over-identified with Black clients, or just troubled. It was as if there were a begrudging acknowledgement of the existence of these issues but they were deemed to have little to do with what was going on in the classroom or curriculum. There was an unquestionably defensive response. There were only 2 courses where these issues were discussed almost exclusively, both taught by Black adjuncts, Racial Transference and Countertransference and a Family Therapy course that often focused on Black families.

---

[11]A classic text on issues of race in the history of psychology, for those interested in the topic, is the following: Guthrie, R. V. (2003). *Even the rat was White: A historical view of psychology* (2nd ed.). Boston: Allyn & Bacon.

Homophobia was a given despite a distinct cohort of lesbian and gay students in each class. Overall if LGB clients were discussed it was via a pathology paradigm and at no point did discussions ever take place, nor did it seem safe to do so, to question the presumption that all psychologists were heterosexual.

There were few discussions about sexual feelings for clients and vice versa, and, oddly, the ones I recall took place in the elective seminar, Racial Transference and Countertransference, where other typically avoided topics were more freely discussed. I would say this was true for practicums as well.

Social class and the impact of class standing on how people viewed themselves were not discussed either. There seemed little awareness of classism and its effects within the therapy process. There were some discussions about patients who *did* not pay but little about how to manage patients who *could* not pay because they perhaps desperately needed but could not afford therapy.

Overall, the issues of power were not addressed, neither the issues of power inequities in society nor the way those issues could be recapitulated in the delivery of psychological services.

Most of the issues that would be incorporated under the heading of diversity or multiculturalism were not addressed. It always seemed ironic that our student body consisted of probably more than the average number of students of color, LGB students, students with visible disabilities, women, people from different class groups, and so on, but none of the issues associated with these identities were discussed. Although there was a clear mandate in the program to include a number of minority students every year, I don't think that was the case for other students from diverse backgrounds that were represented, yet somehow they were there. I think some faculty actively supported this and others did not. Feminist therapy and theory were completely ignored.

That some or all of these topics are now mainstream in some settings, dealt with glancingly or indirectly in others, and still pretty much ignored in others calls attention to an important aspect: Taboos can change over time. And although some tend to be widespread, they often vary from place to place. One program's focus is another's taboo.

The Process of Questioning Myths, Taboos, Secrets, and Uncomfortable Topics

The process we describe in this book avoids a "cookbook" approach that, through a rigid set of steps, brings all readers to the "right" answer to each question and the "right" view of each content area. Each reader is unique in important ways, and each reader's perspective is influenced by experiences, values, and expectations that are unique in important ways. It is not our intent to dictate specific solutions, which would not fit the individual reader and would undercut the book's approach to exploration, discovery, and learning.

Among the keys to this process are a continuing openness to the questions and the differing responses they evoke in each of us. The readiness to question must encompass not only myths, taboos, secrets, and uncomfortable topics but also our own assumptions, habitual ways of thinking about these issues, and "taken for granted" certainties. It is a process of waking up areas where our thinking has become dull and sleepy, and it doesn't end when reaching the last page of this book or the last day of graduate training but, rather, continues throughout our lives. It is a persistent form of careful questioning that examines not only what we're unsure of but also what we're sure of—those facts, theories, and assertions that are most popular, are found in the most authoritative texts, are repeated most often, are most familiar and comforting to us, and seem beyond questioning. It includes a nondefensive openness to being wrong—and to acknowledging that we're fallible and may be wrong—whenever a colleague, a patient, an anomalous fact, a research finding, a new theory, or an unexpected turn of events suggests we may be wrong in our assessment, intervention, ethics, writings, testimony, or any other aspect of our understanding or work.

This persistent questioning can be viewed as a fundamental aspect of psychological science and practice, a view emphasized in chapter 7 as having practical implications for figuring out what to do when we're stuck. This view of persistent questioning as a fundamental aspect of psychological science, for example, was discussed in the *American Psychologist* article "Science as Careful

Questioning." The article illustrated an approach for which the purpose was "not to provide a simplified set of supposed answers or support a sense of certitude but rather to suggest that an essential task of psychologists is careful, informed, and comprehensive questioning" (p. 997).[12,13] As another example, the view of persistent questioning as essential to clinical and counseling psychology is expressed in the following passage:

> This book's approach is not to provide a simplified set of supposed answers, set forth an easy cookbook approach to the ethics of clinical work, or support a sense of certitude but rather to suggest that an essential task of clinical and counseling psychologists is this process of careful, informed, and comprehensive questioning. We must question our own assumptions, biases, and perspectives, not just once during initial training, but throughout our careers. We must also question claims about diagnoses, interventions, and the standard of care, no matter how prestigious or popular the source (p. 71).[14]

This process of questioning continues throughout our lives, and nothing is off-limits.

The Process of Exploration, Discovery, and Learning

This book's process of exploration, discovery, and learning moves from the first chapter to examining an example of the profession's relation to a taboo topic (chap. 2); to discussing conditions in which we can safely explore taboo topics, secrets, and uncomfortable feelings (chap. 3); to a set of questions we'd rather avoid, questions that shed light not only on taboos, secrets, and uncomfort-

---

[12]Pope, K. S. (1997). Science as careful questioning: Are claims of a false memory syndrome epidemic based on empirical evidence? *American Psychologist, 52,* 997–1006; also available at http://kspope.com.

[13]See also Pope, K. S. (1996). Memory, abuse, and science: Questioning claims about the false memory syndrome epidemic. *American Psychologist, 51,* 957–974; also available at http://kspope.com.

[14]Pope, K. S., & Vasquez, M. J. T. (1998). *Ethics in psychotherapy and counseling: A practical guide* (2nd ed.). San Francisco: Jossey-Bass.

able topics but also on what makes us avoid these issues, keep our mouths shut, or change the subject (chap. 4); to looking at frequent clues to unacknowledged topics and feelings (chap. 5); to exploring reactions to the passages and scenarios (chap. 6); and, finally, to a set of seven steps that might help us when we're stuck.

Chapter 2 looks in detail at one of the profession's most widespread, complex, and influential taboos. Sexual feelings about patients—a topic that is different from sexual contact with patients or the ancient prohibition against therapist–patient sexual involvement—were absent from our textbooks for decades. A majority of therapists reported on national surveys that they had experienced one of these sexual feelings—sexual attraction to a patient—and a majority of those who acknowledged sexual attraction reported that the feeling per se (i.e., not acting on the feeling or discussing it with anyone else) tended to make them feel guilty, anxious, and confused. It is still relatively rare that graduate courses in therapy acknowledge and frankly discuss as a common occurrence the range of therapists' sexual feelings (e.g., sexual fantasies about patients, sexual arousal during therapy sessions) and their implications for therapists, patients, and our work. Chapter 2 examines the history of this taboo, what happened when individuals first tried to study the topic, and some of the factors that have worked to keep us silent about it.

2

Therapists' Sexual Arousals, Attractions, and Fantasies: An Example of a Topic That Isn't There

The therapy session focuses on anxiety attacks, but your mind drifts toward what it might be like to have sex with the client. You've worked with a client for over a year and feel such emotional intimacy during the sessions, then find yourself having *very* erotic dreams about the sessions. A client finds you attractive, wears tight pants, and you can see he sometimes has erections during the sessions. You find you enjoy this. A client working on sexual issues describes her sexual fantasies in detail. You find yourself aroused. In the bathtub, you begin to masturbate and find yourself fantasizing about a client. In bed with your partner, you find yourself fantasizing about a client.

Where do we find guidance for situations like these? Over the last 2 decades, there have been a number of books on therapist–patient sexual involvement—how it occurs, its consequences for the therapy and the patient, the legal and ethical standards, and so on—but it's still hard to find books that focus on the sexual feelings of the vast majority of therapists who do *not* become sexually involved with a patient. This is curious because there are so many books in the areas of human sexuality, sex therapies, unethical therapist–patient sexual contact, and management of the patient's sexual behaviors.

Another Myth

This suggests another possible myth: *Good* therapists (i.e., those who don't sexually exploit their patients) never have sexual feelings about their patients, don't become sexually aroused during therapy sessions, don't vicariously enjoy the (sometimes) guilty pleasures of their patients' sexual experiences, and don't have sexual fantasies or dreams about their patients.

The taboo may also draw on the myths mentioned in chapter 1. Therapists may assume that they are invulnerable not only to disease and death but also to their own sexual impulses. They may believe that they would never resort to the cognitive strategies that justify unethical behavior, that, for example, encouraging a very reluctant client to describe arousing sexual fantasies in detail and to repeat the good parts—wait, even better, I'll tape the sessions—that the therapist happens to find arousing to the point of orgasm is sound, and perhaps even cutting-edge, therapy.

This chapter explores the therapist's sexual feelings as an example of a taboo topic, an issue that is often avoided or treated superficially in training programs and practice.

Why has it been so hard to acknowledge, let alone explore and talk about, therapists' sexual feelings? National surveys have suggested that attraction to patients makes most therapists feel guilty, anxious, or confused.[1,2]

These surveys also found that many graduate training programs and internships stopped short of addressing this issue directly and adequately. Most participants in this research reported that their graduate training and internships provided no coverage at all about this topic. Less than 10% reported that their graduate and internship training covered this topic adequately. Subsequent research found that a majority characterized their graduate train-

---

[1]Pope, K. S., Keith-Spiegel, P. C., & Tabachnick, B. G. (1986). Sexual attraction to clients: The human therapist and the (sometimes) inhuman training system. *American Psychologist, 41,* 147–158; also available at http://kspope.com/sexiss/research5.php.

[2]Bernsen, A., Tabachnick, B. G., & Pope, K. S. (1994). National survey of social workers' sexual attraction to their clients: Results, implications, and comparison to psychologists. *Ethics & Behavior, 4,* 369–388.

ing about therapists' feelings of sexual excitement as poor or virtually nonexistent.[3]

What is it about the therapist's sexual reactions to a patient that prompted such extreme avoidance? Why do they make us uncomfortable, and why do we still hesitate to address the topic with the same honesty and openness we ask of our patients? The profession's response to the issue of therapist–patient sex suggests possible reasons that the profession has found it difficult to address therapists' sexual feelings.

Guilt by Association

Sexual feelings for a patient, of course, are *not* the equivalent of sexual involvement with a patient. However, the profession historically showed great resistance to acknowledging the problem of therapist–patient sexual involvement. The veil that covered the problem of sexual behavior with patients also fell over the topic of therapists' sexual feelings. An elaborate Catch-22 evolved: The more sexual feelings about a patient became identified with therapist–patient sex, the less anyone wanted to acknowledge the feelings or discuss the topic in a personal context; the less sexual feelings were acknowledged and discussed as a topic distinct from therapist–patient sex, the more attraction became identified, by default, with therapist–patient sex.

The prohibition against therapist–patient sexual involvement is by no means recent, having been affirmed by Sigmund Freud.[4] The prohibition against physician–patient sexual involvement is even older, having been codified even before the Hippocratic Oath.[5] It is only since the 1970s, however, that the profession be-

---

[3]Pope, K. S., & Tabachnick, B. G. (1993). Therapists' anger, hate, fear, and sexual feelings: National survey of therapist responses, client characteristics, critical events, formal complaints, and training. *Professional Psychology: Research & Practice, 24*, 142–152. This article is reprinted as the appendix of this book.

[4]For quotes from and discussion of Freud's writings on sexual involvement between therapist and patient, please see Pope, K. S. (1994). *Sexual involvement with therapists: Patient assessment, subsequent therapy, forensics*. Washington, DC: American Psychological Association.

[5]Brodsky, A. (1989). Sex between patient and therapist: Psychology's data and response. In G. O. Gabbard (Ed.), *Sexual exploitation in professional relationships*. Washington, DC: American Psychiatric Press.

gan to acknowledge openly violations of the prohibition, to study the incidence and effects of those violations,[6] and to develop ways to help victims.[7]

Attempts to address this topic seemed to reveal professional resistance to publicly acknowledging that violations of the prohibition were occurring. Psychiatrist Clay Dahlberg,[8] for example, who was finally able to publish his article "Sexual Contact Between Patient and Therapist," described the string of editorial rejections that met his attempts to find a publication outlet: "I have had trouble getting this paper accepted. . . . I was told that it was too controversial. What a word for a profession which talked about infantile sexuality and incest in Victorian times" (p. 107).

Seven years later, there still had been so little published on the topic that Virginia Davidson[9] referred, in the title of her article, to the "Problem With No Name." Even in a study published in 1989, Lucille Gechtman[10] explored evidence that resistance to publishing information about social workers who become sexually involved with their clients remained strong among prominent social work associations. Published accounts suggest that there were at least two attempts to gather and make public incidence data on violation of the prohibition prior to Dahlberg's 1970 article. Both attempts ran into resistance.

Martin Shepard[11] described psychologist Harold Greenwald's suggestion, at a meeting of a clinical psychological association, that the association support research into the occurrence of sexual involvement between therapists and their patients. Greenwald described what happened to him as a result of making this sug-

---

[6]Holroyd, J. C., & Brodsky, A. M. (1977). Psychologists' attitudes and practices regarding erotic and nonerotic physical contact with patients. *American Psychologist, 32,* 843–849.

[7]See footnote 4, this chapter.

[8]Dahlberg, C. C. (1970). Sexual contact between client and therapist. *Contemporary Psychoanalysis, 5,* 107–124.

[9]Davidson, V. (1977). Psychiatry's problem with no name. *American Journal of Psychoanalysis, 37,* 43–50.

[10]Gechtman, L. (1989). Sexual contact between social workers and their clients. In G. O. Gabbard (Ed.), *Sexual exploitation in professional relationships* (pp. 27–38). Washington, DC: American Psychiatric Press.

[11]Shepard, M. (1971). *The love treatment: Sexual intimacy between patients and psychotherapists.* New York: Wyden.

gestion in the 1960s: "I just raised the questions . . . intending, as a clinical psychologist, that it be studied like any other phenomenon. And just for raising the question, some members circulated a petition that I should be expelled from the Psychological Association" (p. 2).[12]

Some have questioned whether Greenwald ever made such a statement. Jeffrey Masson,[13] for example, wrote "However, this information comes from Martin Shepard . . . [who] advocates sexual contact with some patients, so it must be taken with a grain of salt" (p. 178). Although Masson's skepticism is not unreasonable, one of the authors of this book (Pope) verified with Greenwald his account.

> Understand that I was only suggesting that we conduct some research, perhaps a survey, on the subject. All I asked was that we take a look at the topic, that we get some data. But there was talk among some members of expelling me. And they cancelled a radio interview. Because I had been scheduled to speak at the convention, those in charge had arranged for one of the radio stations to interview me at the end of the convention. But when they heard what I said, they told me that they had cancelled my interview, that I would not be one of those invited to the scheduled interviews. It was all very strange, but you could see what a nerve this had touched. There was considerable resistance to airing this topic in public. (personal communication)[14]

Another psychologist, Bertram Forer, also attempted to encourage study of therapist–patient sexual involvement in the late 1960s. Obtaining the approval of the Los Angeles County Psychological Association (LACPA) to conduct a formal survey of their membership, Forer started the first systematic research into the rates or frequency with which therapists engage in sex with their patients. Unfortunately, his findings indicated a higher rate of sexual involvement than the research sponsorship had anticipated. On

---

[12]Quoted in Shepard (1971); see footnote 11, this chapter.
[13]Masson, J. M. (1988). *Against therapy*. New York: Atheneum.
[14]H. Greenwald, personal communication to K. Pope, October 1992.

October 28, 1968, the LACPA Board of Directors, after discussing the research data with the associations' leadership, resolved to prohibit presentation of the findings in any public forum (i.e., convention presentation, journal publication, and so on) because it was "not in the best interests of psychology to present it publicly."[15]

Although the Forer data were not permitted to be presented publicly for many years, only a few years later the first article addressing therapist–patient "sexual improprieties" on the basis of systematically collected empirical data was published. This *American Psychologist* article[16] presented analysis and discussion of 10 years' data about professional liability lawsuits filed against psychologists. The database was the records maintained by the insurance carrier that provided liability insurance to members of the American Psychological Association (APA).

Interstingly, this article made no mention of any valid complaint involving a psychologist who had actually engaged in sexual involvement with a patient. Instead, the insurance data were used as the basis for the conclusion

> that the greatest number of [all malpractice] actions are brought by women who lead lives of very quiet desperation, who form close attachments to their therapists, who feel rejected or spurned when they discover that relations are maintained on a formal and professional level, and who then react with allegations of sexual improprieties. (p. 651)[17]

This period reaching into the early 1970s suggests that there may have been considerable resistance in the profession to openly acknowledging and studying violations of the prohibition against therapist–patient sexual involvement. It was not until 1973 that the first survey providing evidence, based on anonymous self-reports of professionals, of sexual contact between therapist and

---

[15]B. Forer, personal communication to K. Pope, January 27, 1993; see also Forer, B. (1980, February). *The psychotherapeutic relationship: 1968.* Paper presented at the annual meeting of the California State Psychological Association, Pasadena.

[16]Brownfain, J. J. (1971). The APA professional liability insurance program. *American Psychologist, 26,* 648–652.

[17]See footnote 16, this chapter.

patient was published[18] and not until 1983 and 1984 that the first studies providing evidence of the harm that can result from those violations were published.[19,20]

Keeping Dirty Laundry Private

Perhaps some of this resistance was based on therapists' shame and embarrassment. The therapy profession claims to help people. It invites the trust of the general public and of the specific people who come, as patients, for help. Many therapists may find it acutely uncomfortable for it to be made public that some members of the profession are exploiting that trust and those patients. Public reports of research or other evidence that some therapists sexually exploit their patients have been described occasionally as airing dirty laundry in public.

"Sensitive Information" About Patients but *Not* About Therapists

When professor Nanette Gartrell, who at that time was at Harvard University, and her colleagues planned an anonymous survey of the membership of the American Psychiatric Association to gather information about psychiatrists' attitudes, beliefs, and behavior in regard to sexual involvement with patients, the association refused to support the research. There appeared to be a stark contrast between the detailed interest taken in eliciting information from and about patients in this area—about victimized patients' possible "promiscuity," sexual history, predisposing clinical con-

---

[18]Kardiner, S. H., Fuller, M., & Mensch, I. N. (1973). A survey of physicians' attitudes and practices regarding erotic and nonerotic contact with patients. *American Journal of Psychiatry, 133,* 1324–1325.

[19]Bouhoutsos, J. C., Holroyd, J., Lerman, H., Forer, B., & Greenberg, M. (1983). Sexual intimacy between psychotherapists and patients. *Professional Psychology: Research and Practice, 14,* 185–196.

[20]Feldman-Summers, S., & Jones, G. (1984). Psychological impacts of sexual contact between therapists or other health care practitioners and their clients. *Journal of Consulting and Clinical Psychology, 52,* 1054–1061.

ditions, problems setting limits, and so on—and the American Psychiatric Association's lack of support for an anonymous survey of its own membership. As the chair of the Ethics Committee of the American Psychiatric Association explained, the association did not believe in asking members for "sensitive information about themselves"(p. 28).[21] Feeling that one's privacy has been invaded, that the spotlight has shifted from the disorders, distress, and actions of the patient to include unflattering characteristics and exploitive behaviors of the therapist, may make many therapists uncomfortable.

Angry, Greedy, Powerful Women and Innocent, Virtuous, Vulnerable Men

The resistance may also reflect a fear of being sued. The claim in the *American Psychologist* article quoted earlier that most suits alleging therapist–patient sex were bogus and came from women leading desperate lives seemed to evolve into a fear of women clients—angry, greedy, powerful, and exploitive—taking advantage of innocent, virtuous, and vulnerable male therapists. The source of the data supposedly demonstrating that most therapist–patient sex claims were made by women of poor character making false claims was the APA Insurance Trust. Rogers Wright,[22] who chaired the trust, described how "consumers recognize the vulnerability of the provider and are attempting to exploit that vulnerability for economic gain"(p. 114). For additional history and documentation of these issues, please see "Therapist–Patient Sex as Sex Abuse: Six Scientific, Professional, and Practical Dilemmas in Addressing Victimization and Rehabilitation."[23]

---

[21]Bass, A. (1989, April 3). Sexual abuse of patients—why?: High incidence may be due to therapists sense of impunity, inaction by professional groups. *Boston Globe*, pp. 27–28.

[22]Wright, R. H. (1985). The Wright way: Who needs enemies? *Psychotherapy in Private Practice, 3,* 111–118.

[23]Pope, K. S. (1990). Therapist–patient sex as sex abuse: Six scientific, professional, and practical dilemmas in addressing victimization and rehabilitation. *Professional Psychology: Research & Practice, 21,* 227–239; also available at http://kspope.com/sexiss/therapy1.php.

Higher Premiums

Another source of resistance may have been a more general concern about economic loss in the form of drastically increased professional liability insurance premiums. During the late 1980s, costs associated with therapist–patient sex claims accounted for about half of all monies paid for claims against psychologists covered by the APA insurance carrier, according to the president of the company.[24] Faced with such actual and potential economic losses, it would not be surprising if therapists were uncomfortable with the topic and ambivalent toward continuing publication of research data that drew increasing public attention to the topic.

"Victimized" by Exclusion?

Although the economic concerns may have potentially affected virtually any therapist, they may have been especially acute for members of the American Psychiatric Association, whose organization had a more direct link to the carrier. Alan Stone,[25] professor of psychiatry and law at Harvard and a former president of the American Psychiatric Association, emphasized that "we should all realize that there is a serious conflict of interest between APA's [American Psychiatric Association's] professional concerns for the victims of sexual exploitation in therapy and its financial concerns when the association's economic interests are at serious risk" (p. 26). He noted that actions taken to eliminate or cap the coverage for sex claims in professional liability policies seemed to violate the profession's commitment for the welfare of its patients.

> Each of us contributes by paying liability insurance to a fund
> that has two functions: to protect us and to compensate those

---

[24]Pope, K. S. (1994). *Sexual involvement with therapists: Patient assessment, subsequent therapy, forensics*. Washington, DC: American Psychological Association.
[25]Stone, A. (1990, March). No good deed goes unpunished. *Psychiatric Times*, pp. 24–27.

who are unfortunate victims of our negligence. With this in mind, the policy decision to exclude victims of sexual exploitation, who are typically women, from participation in our victim compensation fund is difficult to defend. If we are concerned about them, why should they be "victimized" by the exclusion? (p. 25)

Another form of economic loss that may be feared by therapists is that the loss of public trust in the profession would cause a decrease in the number of people seeking therapy.

Are Sexual Feelings Harder to Talk About Than Actual Sexual Involvement?

The intensely negative professional reaction to sexual exploitation of patients may have become associated with all sexual feelings about patients. The reluctance may have been even stronger, however, for the general area of sexual feelings about patients than it has been for sexual contact with patients: Research concerning therapist–patient sexual contact was first published, as previously noted, in 1973; research concerning sexual attraction to patients was not published until 1986. What other factors may account for the profession's seeming reluctance to engage in research on this topic?

Sexual feelings about patients is a topic closer than therapist–patient sexual involvement to most therapists' personal experience and, thus, is more threatening and immediate. Research suggests that sexual feelings about patients are widespread, but relatively few professionals engage in therapist–patient sex. The overwhelming majority of therapists can honestly assure themselves that they are not among those who have violated the prohibition against sexually exploiting patients. Most, however, have felt sexual feelings about or in the presence a patient.

The Altruistic Helper Persona

The topic of sexual feelings about patients calls the public's attention to aspects that may seem discordant with the persona of the therapist as a caring provider of help to those who are in need. Therapists may feel legitimate pride in their altruism and in the services that they provide to those who are hurting. The idea that this altruistic helper may become sexually aroused in the presence of a vulnerable patient may be alarming to the therapist, the patient, and the general public.

Fear of Intrusive Questions

Therapists may be apprehensive that published research on attraction to patients may elicit or invite a patient's questions about the therapist's feelings. Some therapists may feel anxiety at the prospect of a patient asking them, point blank, "Do you find me attractive? Do you ever think about having sex with me? Do you like it when I flirt with you?"

Fear of the Slippery Slope

Therapists may fear that openly acknowledging and publishing works on sexual attraction to patients may somehow increase the likelihood that therapists will engage in sex with patients. The ideas and material are viewed as potentially dangerous to the therapist, to the patient, and to the profession. It is a very human response to attempt to deal with taboo wishes and dangerous temptations by trying to keep them out of awareness. The premise seems to be that if one begins thinking about the forbidden attraction, it will take root, gain force, and thrive, perhaps achieving an uncontrollable life of its own and eventual expression through action. To counter this threat, attempts are made to drive the impulse from awareness, to deny it a foothold in one's thoughts and daydreams, to distract attention from it. But the assumption that trying to ignore and block feelings of attraction will produce the best results for therapists, patients, or the profession is likely no more sound than the discredited fallacy that one should never talk about suicide with a patient because bringing up the topic may "plant the seed" in the person who was not previously suicidal and may overwhelm the suicidal patient, thus increasing the risk that he or she will commit suicide.

Concerns About Context

Therapists may be concerned that material on therapists' sexual feelings may be misused or misconstrued, especially by those who would take it out of context. Such misuse as well as the fear of misuse of sexual material would certainly not be without ample precedent. Adolescents and adults have been known to use anatomy and other medical textbooks not only to satisfy sexual curiosity but also as a source of sexual excitement. Critics have blocked national surveys of child and adolescent sexuality that were to have been undertaken by the U.S. government; citing survey items out of context, critics emphasized their fear that the governmental study of such issues would create the appearance that the government condoned some of the behaviors that were topics of survey items.

Whether adherents or critics of the Freudian tradition, therapists familiar with the history of psychotherapy are aware of the flood of misunderstandings, distortions, and resistance that Freud's attempts to discuss sexual material in the context of psychotherapy encountered not only among many members of the public but also among many of his professional colleagues. Ernest Jones[26] quoted Freud's dismayed reaction to his experience of attempting to discuss his sexual theories at a meeting of the Vienna Neurological Society.

> I treated my discoveries as ordinary contributions to science and hoped to be met in the same spirit. But the silence with which my addresses were received, the void which formed itself about me, the insinuations that found their way to me, caused me gradually to realize that one cannot count upon views about the part played by sexuality ... meeting with the same reception as other communications ... I could not reckon upon objectivity and tolerance. (p. 177)

The reaction to Freud's ideas about sexuality stands as such a vivid scene in the history of psychotherapy that it may be difficult to escape entirely lingering fears that some versions of the

---

[26]Jones, E. (1961). *The life and work of Sigmund Freud* (L. Trilling & S. Marcus, Eds.). New York: Basic Books.

scene may be repeated whenever new areas of sexual exploration are opened.

Anxiety, Guilt, and Embarrassment

Therapists may feel conflicted about the topic of sexual attraction to patients becoming generally recognized as an important part of training programs. As noted in the opening section of this chapter, research suggests that historically the topic has been ignored in most graduate schools and internships. It is not uncommon for therapists-in-training to feel uncomfortable about self-disclosure because they are afraid that they will be criticized or that their disclosures will be viewed as signs of inadequacy as a therapist. The prospect that sexual feelings about patients may become a focus of discussion in classrooms and supervision may intensify that discomfort. Even so senior and prominent a clinician as Harold Searles[27] emphasized the difficulty he had writing about his own sexual reactions to patients. Discussing such reactions, he confessed, "I reacted to such feelings with considerable anxiety, guilt, and embarrassment" (p. 183).

The topic of sexual feelings about patients may be much more complex, uncertain, variable, unpredictable, ambiguous, and elusive than that of therapist–patient sexual involvement. Because of the fundamental differences between sexual feelings and sexual conduct involving patients, exploring sexual feelings may not be as likely to lead to a clear sense of closure, conclusion, or confidence about what will follow as examining the issue of therapist–patient sexual contact. One fundamental difference between sexual feelings about a patient and sexual involvement with a patient, of course, is that a therapist's engaging in sexual activity with a patient is a voluntary behavior on the part of the therapist. As a voluntary behavior, it is something that the therapist can control. By contrast, few would argue that feelings are always or even generally susceptible to voluntary control. That the therapist may at any time be vulnerable to a flow of spontaneous, surprising, and "uncontrolled" feelings may make the topic of

---

[27]Searles, H. F. (1959). Oedipal love in the countertransference. *International Journal of Psychoanalysis, 40,* 180–190.

such feelings much more difficult to address with certainty or confidence.

A second fundamental difference is that the profession has reached a consensus view regarding sexual involvement with patients. That view is "Don't do it. No matter what." There is a clear prohibition against the behavior. Engaging in sex with patients is wrong under any circumstances, it is unethical, and it places patients at risk for harm. On the other hand, the profession does not quite know how to respond to therapists' sexual feelings about their patients. What should a therapist experiencing such feelings do? Aside from redundantly restating the prohibition against sexual contact with patients, there is no consensus about how to respond to such feelings. It would make no sense to encourage or discourage them; they occur, at least for most therapists. Declining even to subject such feelings to research until the mid-1980s, the profession knows relatively little about the topic.

A third fundamental difference, related to the second, is that there is no concrete set of guidelines by which therapists can understand the meaning and implication of feeling sexually attracted to a patient. Sexual involvement with patients violates the prohibition. The accumulated research has enabled the profession to learn something about the frequency of such unethical behavior, the conditions under which it occurs, common characteristics of perpetrators, and possible effects for patients. This research has enhanced the profession's understanding of the negative implications of therapist–patient sex for the therapy. There can be no understanding of the meaning and implications of sexual feelings apart from their relation to the individual therapist and the unique situation, however. Even once the topic is comprehensively researched, it is unlikely that there could ever be a valid "cookbook" that would spell out what sexual feelings meant across different therapeutic situations. The nature, meanings, and implications of sexual feelings about a patient can never be adequately understood apart from the individual therapist, the individual patient, the unique therapeutic situation, and the history and context.

This chapter focused on therapists' sexual feelings as an example of a topic that is taboo; receives only superficial treatment; or provokes anxiety, discomfort, and confusion. Enabling ourselves—as a profession and as individuals—to acknowledge and talk about these topics openly, honestly, and realistically may depend on our willingness to create adequate conditions of learning, the topic of the next chapter.

Chapter

3

Creating Conditions
for Learning

It may be a while before the standard curriculum includes "Introduction to Taboo Topics," "Therapists' Sexual Feelings 101," or "Advanced Secrets and Myths in Psychology Training and Practice," yet the profession must at least try to prepare new professionals to recognize, acknowledge, and confront difficult topics better than we have in the past.

How can we create conditions that will enable us to explore these topics? Ten basic steps provide a good start:

1. Create an environment of safety and trust that encourages honesty, self-examination, and risk taking.
2. Understand that this approach to learning requires self-direction; a departure from situations in which a leader, authority, or textbook "knows the right answer"; self-reflection; and constant questioning.
3. Maintain readiness to disclose uncertain, uncomfortable, vulnerable thoughts and feelings as well as to listen carefully to what others have to say.
4. Nurture respect for all participants.
5. Encourage active participation.
6. Acknowledge everyone's right to privacy.
7. Accept each person's disclosures as viable topics for discussion.
8. Maintain sensitive attention to the nuances of each participant's disclosures.

9. Communicate in a clear, honest manner.
10. Offer support for all participants as they engage in the process of learning and self-exploration.

Discussing these conditions—the degree to which they are present, lingering doubts about them, ways they might be improved in a specific situation, and additional conditions identified by individual participants—may be a useful way for participants to begin a course, workshop, or study group, helping them to get to know each other, develop trust, and create appropriate boundaries and ground rules for their own learning.

Safety

Each participant's sense of safety and basic trust in the integrity of the learning process is a key condition. Not only the teacher, supervisor, or group leader, if there is one, but all participants must take responsibility for creating and maintaining the security of the process.

Exploring topics that may have been taboo, intimidating, or fraught with secrets usually requires actual or perceived risk. Exploring reactions to a hypothetical client or situation may lead to frightening surprises. We may find ourselves thinking the unthinkable or feeling the forbidden. Our responses may strike us as politically incorrect, emotionally incorrect, or just *incorrect*. They may strand us beyond our capacity of self-acceptance. Discovering such personal responses and choosing whether to disclose them can demand considerable courage.

Such risk-taking must be done within a safe and secure environment. For example, participants must believe that what they say will not be used against them, either personally or professionally. It is helpful for a teacher, supervisor, or group leader to emphasize that no adverse consequences will follow, but verbal pronouncements must be supported by moment-to-moment modeling of acceptance of content that emerges. Issues of confidentiality should be discussed at the outset. Whether new members can join the study group once the participants have done the work of establishing a safe context should be addressed early. The concerns surrounding dual roles,[1] when the person who initiates the training is an employer, an internship director, a university instructor giving a grade, or a supervisor who may be called on to write a letter of recommendation, should be carefully and explicitly considered.

Understanding the Task

This book's model of learning probably differs from most of what participants have experienced in graduate-level studies and postgraduate continuing education courses. Participants will not be told or guided toward specific answers as they sometimes are in graduate school, practica, and internships. The model of learning promoted here exposes therapists and therapists-in-training to a wide variety of complex, provocative, or difficult situations; encourages them to tune in to their own responses; and invites mindful awareness, reflection, rethinking, discussion, and questioning.

Openness

The ability of students—whether therapists-in-training or seasoned therapists—to be open to receiving information from others and to disclosing information about themselves is fundamental, because the content of each learning session derives from personal experience and awareness. Note that this requirement for openness serves a different function from that served by openness in personal psychotherapy. In the case of psychotherapy, openness facilitates personal growth and the resolution of problems. In this case, it is important to have representative material for the group to be able to discuss and explore the many implica-

---

[1]For research studies, evolving trends, copies of several of the most widely used decision-making guides (such as Mike Gottlieb's "Avoiding Exploitive Dual Relationships: A Decision-Making Model" and Jeff Younggren's eight-step model "Ethical Decision-Making & Dual Relationships"), and relevant articles from the *American Psychologist* and other professional journals, see the section Dual Relationships & Boundary Dilemmas: Trends, Stats, Guides, and Resources at http://kspope.com/dual/dual.php.

tions of taboo or uncomfortable topics in therapy. The material that each learning group will explore is the variety of feelings and other reactions evoked by reading the passages and scenarios in chapter 6 as well as the questions following each segment.

Respect

Valuing both the person and the person's contribution to the learning process is easily threatened in this type of situation, because a principal goal is to explore uncharted waters. People reveal a lot about themselves, even when discussing hypothetical cases. The possibility that differences in attitudes, feelings, and experiences may be perceived as defects, deviance, immaturity, character flaws, ignorance, prejudice, psychopathology, or traits incompatible with being a therapist can be discussed before learning exercises are undertaken. Using one of the passages in chapter 6 (e.g., those by Harold Searles[2] or Helen Block Lewis[3]) for discussion of respect for the self-disclosing person might be helpful.

Although respect for disclosing participants is a prerequisite for learning in this area, it is possible that this learning process will also strengthen participants' inclination to respect peers for exploration of their responses to controversial, taboo, or difficult topics and to refrain from our all-too-common tendency to label, dismiss, attack personally, demean, engage in ad hominem, and disparage those with whom we disagree.

Encouragement

People in the study group will likely vary in the amount of encouragement required to enter into this learning activity. Especially when the material is threatening, many of us would dearly love to learn vicariously rather than through immediate experi-

---

[2]Searles, H. F. (1959). Oedipal love in the countertransference. *International Journal of Psychoanalysis, 40,* 180–190.

[3]Lewis, H. B. (1971). *Shame and guilt in neurosis.* Madison, CT: International Universities Press.

ence. But exploring our responses to and feelings about these sometimes difficult, taboo, or troublesome topics cannot be a passive or secondhand experience. It is not something that can be reasoned out from reading basic texts on theory or pieced together from research data.

Learning groups and their leaders must confront honestly the issue of motivation—or lack of motivation—to participate in the learning process. Some teachers or students may not have made a voluntary choice to enter the group. Participation may be required by the graduate training program, internship, or employing agency providing in-service training. Departmental chairs, training directors, or executive offices may have "volunteered" some faculty or staff for this course. All participants must confront honestly why they are in this learning group and the ways in which the setting, the participants, and the process can best offer nonintrusive, gentle encouragement of a safe and useful learning experience.

Privacy

Participants need to know that they are the arbiters of what they will or won't disclose, without pressure to bare their souls more than would be comfortable or agreeable. Unlike sensitivity groups, the goal is not to teach people to be less defensive with peers. In addition to explicit statements about everyone's rights not to reveal personal material, the structure of the learning experience can be used to reduce implicit pressure for self-disclosure. For example, participants may be given the opportunity to deal with some, but not all, of the passages and scenarios in chapter 6. All participants and group leaders must be sensitive to the fact that what one person at one time may feel as "encouragement" (as discussed in the previous section), another person (or the same person at another time) may feel as intrusiveness, pressure, or intimidation.

Acceptance

To be able to discuss the implications of various kinds of therapist responses to topics that are sometimes controversial, difficult, or taboo, it is necessary to promote discussion of a very wide variety of feelings, attitudes, and behaviors. Chapter 6 presents first-person anecdotes that may stir emotions. Many readers' reactions probably would not, by the wildest stretch of the imagination, be considered "acceptance" of what some therapists in the anecdotes are described as experiencing or doing. The challenge, however, is to maintain mindful awareness of these immediate feelings (e.g., fear, anxiety, anger, confusion, disgust), to acknowledge, reflect on, and discuss them. There must be readiness to encounter and explore content that at times provokes negative or rejecting reactions, and a readiness to explore those reactions so that exploration, discovery, reflection, questioning, and learning can occur. The same would hold true, and even more so, for material presented from the participants' own experiences.

There are two caveats that apply to learning the "acceptance of content" process, one obvious and one subtle. Obviously, acceptance or receptivity to someone's attitudes, feelings, thoughts, and fantasies does not imply that one would decide to act along the lines of those feelings. For example, acceptance (receptivity) toward someone who suggests that cradling, rocking, and stroking an affection-deprived patient is therapeutic does not imply that one would eventually include that in one's repertoire, but it does imply that one can discuss the pros and cons openly and attempt to explore and understand the meanings and implications of this intervention.

Another example, this one from a different context, may be useful. A client may confront a therapist with suicidal feelings, intent, and plans. Rather than reflexively rejecting the client's feelings and stated goal (i.e., to commit suicide), the therapist may explore this frightening, final, and "unacceptable" option with the client. The client may discuss in detail the pain and confusion that led to this choice, the client's methods for ending his or her life, anticipations or fantasies about what it would be like to die and to be dead, ideas about how the act might affect others, the relief and other positive feelings the client may experience when thinking about ending all suffering and problems, and the deeply textured meanings of bringing one's life to an end. The therapist's careful attention to and acceptance of the client's feelings, intentions, and fantasies and the exploration and discovery that therapist and client conduct together does not mean that the therapist believes that suicide is the best or even an acceptable alternative. In some cases, such exploration and discovery may be the most effective way to reduce the risk that the client will commit suicide. Acceptance, as used in this section, refers to the acknowledgment of and willingness to explore areas of human experience that may evoke anxiety, fear, guilt, disgust, outrage, and an almost infinite variety of other human reactions. It refers to the acknowledgment of and willingness to explore these areas in ourselves as well as in others.

Less obviously, there is a tendency for therapists to intellectualize or objectify in extreme degree our feelings in this area to avoid the emotional work involved in acknowledging, exploring, and understanding associated issues. Resorting to cool rationality in dealing with this material too quickly or too exclusively— that is, if we slap a quick or impressive-sounding label on something as a substitute for feeling, thinking, and questioning, we succeed only in avoiding the learning that is possible in this process.

Sensitivity

In addition to being receptive toward reading or hearing about topics that are sometimes taboo, controversial, or difficult, participants will need to improve their perceptive and expressive skills. This is where those qualities that many therapists value— empathy and accurate perception—come in. If a patient says, "I really want to go to bed with you," what are the many dimensions, complexities, and implications of this communication? If a group participant acknowledges, "That patient's statement would make me feel [hopeless, horny, jealous, homicidal]," can the others hear the communication with the same sensitive appreciation for levels and ambiguities of meaning that they hope to provide for their patients?

The same attention to sensitivity must occur when group members address each other with clarifying statements, questions, and so on. From the start, participants must take responsibility for not shaming, demeaning, or threatening other group members in the way they talk with them. This is a distinct departure from the more free-flowing group therapy situation in which confrontation and even abrasiveness among group members are simply more grist for the mill. The fundamental goal is not to learn to manage the tension arising from interpersonal interactions but to learn about the breadth, depth, variety, and effects of our personal and professional responses to these complex topics.

Frankness

A sensitive way of expressing one's thoughts, observations, and feelings should not interfere with clear and honest communication. Frank communication probably emerges from several other items on this list of prerequisites—respect, openness, and acceptance in particular. Occasionally a study group may be so concerned with protecting the welfare of its members that it doesn't permit open discussion of potentially disruptive material. Periodically asking the members to attend to what is *not* being mentioned or addressed may be helpful. In graduate school, therapy, a study group, or any other setting, a powerful central issue can influence or even dominate discussion, yet we may act as if the issue did not exist. We may discuss an issue using euphemisms, jargon, or other language that works more to conceal, distort, or misdirect than communicate. Speaking the truth, at least as we understand it, to ourselves and others is an essential step in this model of exploration and learning.

Support

Finally, a supportive attitude on the part of the course or learning group leader, if there is a leader, and on the part of each member can make the difference between a process that works and one that essentially just passes time. The nature of the material often provokes anxiety, and discussions involve real or perceived risks for the participants. In helping therapists and therapists-in-training to engage in this kind of exploration, discovery, and learning, support helps reduce tension, create a rich database for consideration, and enable exploration, discovery, and learning.

Therapists and therapists-in-training who have engaged in this kind of exploration, discovery, and learning have often described it as some of the most difficult yet productive, rewarding, and transformative educational work that they've done. The process is not easy. Plenty of factors make us look away from these topics, block awareness of our responses, and lead us to assume that exploration and questioning are better avoided. Acknowledging and accepting the impulse to shy away from these areas are often points of departure as well as part of the learning process suggested in this book. The process involves attempting to be relentlessly honest about ourselves, our feelings, our thoughts, and our responses. It involves allowing ourselves to become vulnerable as we learn about our vulnerabilities. It provides an opportunity for a self-assessment, which is the focus of the next chapter.

4

Questions We'd Rather Avoid: A Self-Assessment

So far we've yet to encounter any clinician who reports studying at a graduate school, practicum, or internship in which there were no secrets, taboo topics, or subjects that students, professors, or supervisors didn't stay a good distance away from. Most educational and training institutions where people learn how to do therapy seem to have not only the proverbial "elephant in the middle of the room" that no one mentions but also a herd of giraffes, a mustering of storks, a flock of turkeys, a knot of toads, some lions and tigers and bears (oh my!), a few sacred cows, and, almost always, a grouse.

This chapter invites you to try a self-assessment, using your own experience as a way of learning about the secrets, taboos, and uncomfortable topics that seem to lurk in virtually all clinical training programs. This process of questioning can also teach us about factors that encourage us to avoid these issues, keep our mouths shut, or change the subject. Confronting these questions lays the groundwork for the more extensive explorations later in the book and is useful preparation for creating, leading, or participating in a study group on these topics.

The challenge for any of us is to explore these issues with thoughtfulness, frankness, and sensitivity, while avoiding censoring ideas, quashing feelings, or rushing through the questions in this chapter without feeling and thinking. Our responses to some of these questions may strike some—including ourselves—

as confused or confusing, "politically incorrect," "emotionally incorrect," ignorant, small-minded, biased, insulting, intolerant, prejudiced, dangerous, or a sure sign that we are not fit to be therapists. That our responses might elicit such critical responses may be a clue to why the topics are often avoided.

This self-assessment is likely to be useful only to the extent that we can be honest about our responses. Keeping in mind the previous chapter's 10 basic learning conditions may be helpful.

Questions

What was the most difficult thing you ever told a therapy supervisor? Why was it difficult?

Was there ever anything you decided either not to tell your therapy supervisor or to tell only in "edited" form?

In your graduate program, practica, or internship, was there any topic that seemed to be taboo or uncomfortable to address, that either went unmentioned or was talked about in the most superficial, stilted, or abstract terms? If so, what was it?

In your graduate program, practica, or internship, did you ever regret having brought up a topic, disclosed something, or taken a stance? If so, what was it, and why did you regret it?

In your graduate program, practica, or internship, what factors—including different kinds of individual dynamics, social or cultural factors, interpersonal dynamics, group process, organizational structure—seemed to foster secrets, taboos, and avoidance of important topics?

For you personally, what factors seem to foster secrets, taboos, and avoidance of important topics?

In your graduate program, practica, or internship, in what ways, if any, could openness, directness, and honesty be a liability?

In your graduate program, practica, or internship, what, if anything, could not be questioned?

In your graduate program, practica, or internship, was anyone ever penalized in any way for questioning an assumption, an approach, a rule, a professor, a supervisor, or anyone or anything else? If so, how were they penalized and for what?

In your graduate program, practica, or internship, were any patients ever disparaged, ridiculed, or spoken about in a disrespectful manner when they were not present? If so, how would you characterize the patients who were the objects of these comments? Did they share any common characteristics?

In your graduate program, practica, or internship, were any students ever disparaged, ridiculed, or spoken about in a disrespectful manner when they were not present? If so, how would you characterize the students who were the objects of these comments? Did they share any common characteristics?

If patients or students were ever disparaged, ridiculed, or spoken about in a disrespectful manner in your graduate program, practica, or internship, did that play any role in shaping what could and could not be said, acknowledged, or questioned?

In your graduate program, practica, or internship, was there any competitiveness (stop laughing!)? In what ways, if any, did the competitiveness play a role in shaping what could and could not be said, acknowledged, or questioned?

What other factors beside competitiveness, if any, played a role in shaping what could and could not be said, acknowledged, or questioned?

In your graduate program, practica, or internship, did you or any of your peers ever discuss feelings of incompetence, of being in over your head, of feeling overwhelmed or confused? In what context? How were such discussions received or handled and by whom?

In your graduate program, practica, or internship, did any of your supervisors ever discuss feeling incompetent, overwhelmed, or confused? In what context? How were such discussions received or handled?

Have you ever blushed or become embarrassed when you were with a therapy or counseling client? Why?

What, if anything, could a client say or do to you that would be uncomfortable or embarrassing to you during the session?

What, if anything, could a client say or do to you that you'd be uncomfortable or embarrassed to tell your supervisor about?

What, if anything, could a client say or do to you that you'd be uncomfortable or embarrassed putting in the client's chart?

What has a client said or done that has upset you the most?

Could you still work effectively with a client with whom you were upset?

Have you ever made a mistake with a client because you were upset with the client?

What, if anything, has a client said or done or could a client say or do that would make you hate the client?

Have you ever worked with a client you hated? If so, could you work effectively with that client?

What, if anything, has a client said or done or what could a client say or do that would frighten you?

Have you ever worked with a client who frightened you? If so, could you work effectively with that client?

What, if anything, has a client said or done, or what could a client say or do, that you would experience as sexually arousing?

Have you ever worked with a client whom you experienced as sexually arousing? If so, could you work effectively with that client?

Under what circumstances would the client know that you were sexually aroused?

Under what circumstances would you disclose your arousal to the client?

Under what circumstances would you disclose your arousal to your supervisor?

Under what circumstances would you mention your arousal in your notes?

What, if anything, could a client do that you would find disgusting?

Have you ever worked with a client whom you experienced as disgusting? If so, could you work effectively with that client?

Under what circumstances would the client know that you were disgusted?

Under what circumstances would you disclose your disgust to the client?

Under what circumstances would you disclose your disgust to your supervisor?

Under what circumstances would you mention your disgust in your notes?

Can you remember a time during a therapy session that you became privately but intensely aware of your own body? What seemed to lead to this awareness?

Can you remember a time during a therapy session when your bodily processes (e.g., a burp, a stomach rumble) became obvious not only to you but also to your client? How did you respond?

During a therapy session, have you ever had the impulse to get up and move about (e.g., to stretch, to relieve the tension in your arms and legs, to help you "wake up")? How did you respond to this impulse?

During a therapy session, have you ever fallen asleep or felt very close to falling asleep? How did you respond?

Are there any client physical types, characteristics, or disabilities that make you uncomfortable in any way?

How were issues of physical disabilities discussed in your graduate program, practica, or internship? Were the discussions, in your opinion, honest, helpful, and adequate? Were any aspects of physical disabilities "off limits"?

In your graduate program, practica, or internship, were there any barriers to access for people with disabilities?

Under what circumstances would you hold a client's hand?

Under what circumstances would you put your arm around a client?

Under what circumstances would you cradle a client's head in your lap?

Under what circumstances would you hug a client?

Have you ever hugged a client or been hugged by a client in such a way that seemed to have sexual overtones for you or the client? What did you feel? What did you do?

Has a client ever initiated a hug or kiss that you did not want? What feelings did it evoke? How did you handle the situation?

Under what circumstances would you kiss a client on the cheek or forehead?

Under what circumstances would you kiss a client on the mouth?

Under what circumstances would you have dinner with a client?

Under what circumstances would you go to a client's home?

Under what circumstances would you enter a client's bedroom?

Has a client ever dressed in a way that made you uncomfortable? What was the nature of your discomfort? How did you respond to feelings of discomfort?

Have you ever imagined what a client's body would look like if he or she were not wearing any clothes? What feelings did this imaginary scene evoke in you? Do you think the client was ever aware that you were creating this imaginary scene? If he or she had been aware, what feelings do you think it might have evoked in him or her?

Do you believe that a client has ever imagined what your body would look like if you were not wearing any clothes? What feelings does this evoke in you?

Has a client ever touched his or her genitals in your presence? What feelings did this evoke in you?

What is the most private part of a client's body that you have seen? How did your viewing this part of his or her body come about? Has a private part of a client's body ever been exposed to you through apparent accident (e.g., a man's gym shorts shift to reveal he is not wearing underwear; a woman's low-cut blouse slides down)? Was it apparent to the client that a private part of his or her anatomy was exposed? Was it apparent to the client that you noticed? Did either you or the client mention the incident? What feelings did it seem to evoke in the client? What feelings did it evoke in you?

Has a client ever talked about his or her sexual experiences or fantasies in a way that you found enjoyable? What feelings did they evoke in you? Do you think that the client was aware of your enjoyment? If so, how do you think this awareness might have affected or influenced the client?

Have you ever had an erotic dream about a client? Did you pay any particular attention to the dream once you awoke?

Have you ever been so upset over something that has happened in therapy or so concerned about a patient that it interfered with your sex life?

Have you ever become aware of a client's body odor? What feelings did this evoke in you? How did you respond to those feelings?

Have you ever fantasized about a client while you masturbated or had sex with someone else (who was not your client)? Did you reflect on the fantasy later? Did your awareness of the fantasy affect the therapy or your relationship with the client? Did you have any positive reactions to your fantasy (e.g., excitement, pride, curiosity)? Did you have any negative reactions to your fantasy (e.g., anxiety, guilt, fear, uncomfortable confusion)?

Have you ever had a sexual fantasy or daydream during a therapy session? Did it involve the client? Did it seem to have any meaning for the therapy or for your relationship to the client?

Has a client ever seemed to become sexually aroused or excited in your presence? What seemed to cue you to your client's arousal?

What feelings did that evoke in you? How, if at all, was the arousal discussed?

Has a client ever told you that he or she was sexually attracted to you? What feelings did that evoke in you?

Try to remember a client who told you that he or she was sexually attracted to you but whom you did not find yourself attracted to, and another client who told you he or she was sexually attracted to you and to whom you were attracted. (If you have not experienced both situations, try to create the situations in your imagination.) Does whether you're attracted make any difference in how you respond to the two clients? Do you believe that either of the two clients could intuit whether you were attracted to him or her?

During a counseling session with a client, have you ever had feelings of which you were ashamed? How did you respond to those feelings? Have you ever experienced a reaction to a client that you were too ashamed to tell to anyone else?

During a counseling session with a client, have you ever done anything of which you were ashamed? What happened?

Does a client's sexual orientation evoke any particular feelings in you? Does it affect how you respond to a client's discussion of sexual attraction to you?

Does your sexual orientation affect your responses to clients' physical attributes? Does it affect your responses to clients' discussions of sexual feelings or behaviors? If so, how?

How were issues of sexual orientation discussed in your graduate program, practica, or internship? Were the discussions, in your opinion, honest, helpful, and adequate? Were any aspects of sexual orientation "off limits"?

Have you ever reacted to a client's sexual talk or behavior with anger?

Have you ever reacted to a client's sexual talk or behavior with fear?

Have you ever reacted to a client's sexual talk or behavior with anxiety?

Have you ever reacted to a client's sexual talk or behavior with guilt?

Have you ever reacted to a client's sexual talk or behavior with embarrassment?

Have you ever reacted to a client's sexual talk or behavior with intense curiosity?

Have you ever been concerned that a client might file a false complaint against you for sexual misconduct? What led you to become concerned? How did this concern affect the way you conducted therapy? How did this concern affect the way you felt about the client?

Do you talk about sexual issues more with your male clients, your female clients, or both about equally?

Do you touch your male clients more, your female clients more, or both about equally?

What are the proportions of men and women among your clientele? Is that due to chance, to the general distribution of male and female clients in your geographic area (or clinic), or to other factors? Do you wish you had more male clients or more female clients?

Do you generally find yourself more sexually attracted to people of a certain race or ethnicity? If so, what implications might this have for the way you conduct therapy?

Do you find yourself feeling more positive toward some races and ethnicities and more negative toward others? How, if at all, does this affect your work as a therapist?

What discussions in your graduate program, practica, or internship involved issues of race or ethnicity? Were the discussions, in your opinion, honest, helpful, and adequate? Were any aspects of race and ethnicity "off limits"?

Under what conditions would you discuss your own sexual fantasies with a client?

Under what conditions would you show a client how to put on a condom?

Under what conditions would you show a client how to insert a tampon?

Under what conditions would you examine a female client's chest and nipples?

Under what conditions would you examine a male client's chest and nipples?

Under what conditions would you allow a client to disrobe partially during a session?

Under what conditions would you allow a client to disrobe completely during a session?

Under what conditions would you partially disrobe during a session?

Under what conditions would you completely disrobe during a session?

Do you ever cry or "tear up" during therapy sessions? If so, what has the client said or done? Does this seem to happen more with male clients, more with female clients, about equally with male and female clients?

Have you ever hit, slapped, or pushed a client? What were the circumstances?

Have you ever felt like hitting, slapping, or pushing a client? What were the circumstances?

With what client have you felt most intimate? How did you express the intimacy?

In your graduate school, practica, or internship, did you ever do anything with a client that you were reluctant to mention to your supervisor? Did you ultimately reveal or refrain from revealing this matter to the supervisor? What were your reasons for making this choice?

In your graduate school, practica, or internship, did you ever find that the sexual feelings, anger, hate, fear, or upset in the therapy you conducted were reflected in some way in your relationship to your supervisor? If so, how did you respond?

At what time while you were doing psychotherapy did you feel the most emotional intensity? Would you describe it as a positive or negative emotional experience? What evoked this intensity? How did you respond to it?

Under what circumstances do you avoid recording sexual material in a client's chart?

Have you ever told a sexual partner about one of your clients? Did this include talking about sexual material? Do you believe that the client was aware of the possibility that you might be discussing him or her with your sexual partner? How do you believe the client would feel were he or she to know that you had had such discussions with your sexual partner?

If you could be given an absolute assurance that you would suffer no negative consequences (e.g., no one else would ever know, there would be no complaint to a licensing board, ethics committee, civil court, or criminal court), would you ever consider entering into a sexual relationship with one of your clients? What factors would you take into account in your considerations? What would you decide?

If your clients could, beginning right now, read your mind—including, but not limited to, all the thoughts and feelings you've had about them—what thought or feeling would be most surprising to them?

If your clinical supervisors in graduate school, practica, or internship could, beginning right now, read your mind—including, but not limited to, all the thoughts and feelings you've had about them—what thought or feeling would be most surprising to them?

What comment could a client make about your looks, sexuality, or other personal aspects that you would find most hurtful?

Do you believe that it is possible that you may have acted seductively, fearfully, angrily, or hatefully toward a client without your being aware of it?

Have you ever felt jealous of a client's life partner, sexual partner, or dating partner?

Have you ever felt jealous of a client for other reasons?

If there are certain kinds of clients who make you uncomfortable, how would you describe them? How, if at all, does your discomfort affect your ability to work effectively with them? To what extent is your discomfort acknowledged or reflected in your notes?

Does any aspect of your own abilities or limitations as a therapist make you uncomfortable? How do you respond to this discomfort?

Has any aspect of your identity, development, and work as a therapist been particularly hard for you to acknowledge to yourself or others? If so, why do you think it was so difficult to acknowledge, and what did you do about it?

✛ ✛ ✛

How hard was it to stay focused and respond to each question openly and honestly? Were you able to maintain a mindful awareness of your thoughts and feelings in response to each question? If not, what factors pushed your awareness away from the task? Which questions were most important and personally meaningful to you?

5

Possible Clues to Taboo Topics and Uncomfortable Feelings

Clients—and sometimes therapists—can idealize therapists as always aware of their own feelings and never turning away from taboo topics. But as imperfect humans, we can get caught off guard, tripped up by unexamined habits, accidental oversights, unrealistic expectations, and life's tendency to surprise us.

This chapter briefly discusses 17 *possible* clues gathered from our professional experiences that may help a therapist become aware when taboo topics, unacknowledged feelings, or other unidentified or misidentified factors are affecting the therapist, the client, or the therapy process.

In any given situation, of course, these clues may reflect factors completely unrelated to the themes of this book. In our experiences, however, they are always worth paying attention to and often are associated with myths, taboos, or uncomfortable feelings. Like the previous chapter, what follows involves self-assessment. You are encouraged to "try on" each of the clues to see if any of them fit.

The 17 possible clues are as follows:

- ☐ Therapy adrift
- ☐ Repetitive therapy
- ☐ The discrepant record
- ☐ The dehumanized client
- ☐ The dehumanized therapist

☐ Avoidance
☐ Theory-obliterated therapy
☐ The client–friend
☐ Obsession
☐ Interesting slips and meaningful mistakes
☐ Fantasies, dreams, daydreams, and other imaginings
☐ Undue special treatment
☐ Isolation of the client
☐ Isolation of the therapist
☐ Creating a secret
☐ Seeking repeated reassurance from colleagues
☐ Boredom and drowsiness as protective reactions

Each theoretical orientation may have its own assumptions and terminology for understanding why and how these phenomena occur, their implications, and the ways they are best addressed.

The clues are described only briefly not only because there is nothing elaborate or mysterious about how they work but also because they are so blatantly obvious, at least if you are not currently experiencing them. They are the kind of experience that, when presented to a consultant, suggest immediately that something is going on that needs attention.

When we look back on our own experiences with such clues, we tend to find them signals of exceptional clarity . . . at least in hindsight. Yet it is easy to miss these clues if it is we who are currently experiencing them. For that reason, we provide these examples in the form of a brief list, with minimal discussion. If therapists can hold these constantly in mind and check from time to time to see whether any of them are present, it can serve as an early-warning system.

It is worth reemphasizing that any of these clues, when occurring at a particular time in a particular situation, may reflect something other than a taboo topic, unacknowledged feeling, or other unidentified or misidentified factor. In our experience as therapists and therapy supervisors, however, attending to these clues tends to be helpful to therapists, increasing understanding of important aspects of the therapy, uncovering factors that are blocking or slowing the therapeutic process, and preventing problems.

Therapy Adrift

If there is a powerful factor or taboo topic that the therapist alone or the therapist and client are working to avoid noticing, identifying, or addressing, the therapy may drift aimlessly. Therapist and client continue to meet and to discuss topics that seem important, but there is no movement toward the client's stated goals, developmental progress, or increased understanding. There tends to be no discussion of the degree to which the client is—or is not—making progress on what lead him or her to seek therapy in the first place, no evaluation of what is and is not working. Therapy seems to just float without direction, as if it were resting atop the water somewhere in the middle of an ocean. One therapist noticed that therapy had drifted for the first 6 months of treatment. On reflection, and with the help of consultation, it became clear to her that the client had sought therapy for his self-destructive impulses, but the prospect that if they discussed self-destructiveness the client might become suicidal and take his own life terrified the therapist. She had lost a client to suicide the previous year and found it almost impossible to admit to herself that she no longer felt competent to work with suicidal clients.

Repetitive Therapy

If therapy adrift seems aimless and directionless, repetitive therapy tends to be frustratingly predictable in the ground it covers because it seems to cover the same ground each session or each small group of sessions. Some clients make a specific gain on a regular basis, only to see the progress routinely lost. Others make a naïve and unrealistic assessment of new friends, romantic relationships, family life, or employment. Therapy sessions focus on the seemingly endless repetition of a cycle: an idealizing assessment followed by shattered assumptions. Still others come in each week with a new and "completely unexpected" crisis that has thrown life into chaos. And so on.

However diverse the patterns, the common characteristic is that the pattern is constantly repeated in therapy. A therapist finally mentioned a case she'd been reluctant to discuss with her peer-consultation group. The therapy was almost in its third year with virtually no real progress. Each month or so, the client and therapist would plan how the client could bring about changes in her life, and the client would earnestly set about taking those steps. Within a few weeks, however, there would be what the client described as a "blowup" at home, and her plans became lost in the chaos. With the encouragement, support, and help of the peer-consultation group, the therapist began to acknowledge that it was the client's violently abusive partner who caused the blow-ups. Both the client and the therapist were frightened of the partner's potential for violence, kept it out of awareness, and avoided this topic, and this undermined the therapy.

The Discrepant Record

Significant discrepancies between what is recorded in the client's chart and what is actually happening in therapy can be a possible clue to taboo topics, uncomfortable feelings, and unidentified or misidentified factors affecting the therapist, the client, or the therapy. Well-written clinical records tend to provide a good, or at least adequate, sense of the client and the therapy. A discrepant record is off track, with the recorded data obscuring the essentials and misleading or confusing the reader. When looking over their prior records after coming to terms with a taboo topic, therapists have described their writings as disengaged ("What I wrote was rote."), a pack of clichés, and sometimes even confabulation. One White therapist working with a African American in a therapy in which race was the great unmentionable later discovered that in records for 5 months of therapy, the topic of race was completely absent except for one mention: When describing the client's demographics after the intake session, the therapist had mistakenly described the client as White.

The Dehumanized Client

When work with a client threatens to bring up feelings that are too uncomfortable, one protective step therapists can take is to dehumanize the client. If, for example, the client is dealing with losses that echo too loudly in the therapist's own life and put the therapist at risk for feeling "too emotional," "too sad," or somehow overwhelmed, the therapist can turn the real person who is the patient into a diagnosis (e.g., "that schizophrenic," "the borderline personality disorder I'm treating"). The client disappears and becomes only a few dysfunctions, symptoms, or labels. A therapist who considered himself "antireligion" suddenly realized, months into therapy, that he had lost all sense of connection with a client and was referring to that client only in abstract terms. Reflecting on this lack of connection, which he was not experiencing with any of his other patients, he discovered that the nature of the client's religious struggles were striking a meaningful—but very unwanted—chord in the therapist. Dehumanizing the client helped the therapist avoid addressing, in a direct and immediate way, material that was threatening the therapist's antireligion stance.

The Dehumanized Therapist

In this strategy, the therapist attempts to drain away his or her humanity rather than that of the client. The therapist may begin acting like a wise and distant computer, emitting observations, wisdom, or advice as neutrally as possible. The therapist may start using jargon and technical terms to the exclusion of more immediate, everyday words. In supervision or consultation, the therapist may talk and function exclusively on an intellectual, rational, or theory-driven level, avoiding all but the most perfunctory and superficial reference to feelings, impulses, or spontaneous reactions. Conceptualizations, terminology, and interventions seem to hold the therapist's feelings at bay (i.e., from the therapist's own awareness) rather than to enable the therapist to respond helpfully to the person who is the client.

Avoidance

If work with a client involves a taboo topic or uncomfortable feelings, one of the most obvious strategies to avoid the taboo or discomfort is to avoid the client. Suddenly reasons to cancel sessions or reduce the frequency of regularly scheduled sessions flood the therapist's mind. The therapist finds that miscommunications lead to missed sessions. The therapist records the wrong time or date for the next appointment or forgets that a session has been scheduled. The therapist may try to avoid any thoughts of the patient or may mentally cast about to see whether there might be a reason to transfer the patient to someone else. Or perhaps it's time to terminate! If the therapist meets with a supervisor each week to discuss five current clients, the therapist may find that there is only enough time, as the weeks pass, to discuss the other four patients; the avoided patient tends to slip through the cracks, remaining unmentioned or receiving only quick, perfunctory mention at the end of the supervisory session. If the patient talks of termination, the therapist may immediately and without clinical rationale encourage this option, avoiding discussion of reasons, consequences, or meanings. If the patient terminates abruptly and without notice, the therapist may simply write "patient terminated" in the chart and make no real effort to contact the patient.

Theory-Obliterated Therapy

If work with a particular client threatens the therapist with topics that are taboo, feelings that seem too intense, or issues that run afoul of myths, therapists may try to make the client and therapy disappear within a theory. The therapists may, for example, select some tangential themes mentioned by the client, frame the therapy around those themes, and use a theoretical orientation to guide the sessions. One therapist met on a weekly basis with a client for 3 months, and both the clinical record and the therapist's sessions with a supervisor showed an impressive grasp of theory and steady movement toward a sequence of therapeutic goals. What was overlooked was what had prompted the client to seek therapy: questions about sexual orientation. The client, married with 3 young children, had begun to experience an intense romantic and sexual attraction to someone of the same sex and had sought counseling to obtain information, reassurance, and support in exploring the nature, meaning, and implications of this attraction and whether to act on it. The topic, however, was threatening to the therapist, who helped guide the client's attention to other, easier-to-discuss issues. The client offered no resistance to this diversion because the topic was threatening to the patient as well as the therapist.

The Client–Friend

A therapist anxious about a client, therapy, or unresolved personal issues can avoid the anxiety by transforming the client into a friend and replacing professional responsibilities with an interesting version of friendship in which one "friend" pays the other "friend" for the friendship. The sessions can take on the give-and-take of two friends meeting over coffee, catching up on whatever is going on in their lives, discussing current events, and passing the time in a way that is enjoyable for both. Some meetings may move from the office to restaurants, the bridge table, the tennis court, or the neighborhood bar.

One therapist joined a peer-consultation group after conducting a solo private practice for 2 years. As each of the members of the group discussed their work, he became aware, as did others, that although he'd been passing the time with his clients in interesting ways that were pleasurable to both therapist and client, no therapy had been taking place and none of the patients had made any progress beyond locating the best restaurants in the neighborhood, learning strategies for conducting a grand slam in no trump, improving the backhand cross-court kill shot, discovering the secrets to obscure bar bets, and so on. As he continued to discuss his situation with the trusted members of his peer-consultation group, he became aware that he had felt like a fraud in graduate school, never felt competent to do therapy, and wanted to avoid the anxiety-provoking responsibilities of actual psychotherapy. He was much more comfortable with "friends" than with clients. In his relatively brief 2 years of experience, he had developed countless rationalizations and elaborate theoretical justifications, for which he argued vigorously, to escape a role for which he felt inadequate.

With the nonjudgmental acceptance and support of his consultation group, he was able to acknowledge and work through the implications of his fear of professional responsibilities.

Obsession

Obsession with a client is one of the most vivid examples of a situation in which the clue to unacknowledged taboos, secrets, or uncomfortable feelings can be instantly apparent to those (e.g., a supervisor, consultant, or colleague) to whom the therapist makes the clue known but difficult to decipher for the therapist who experiences the obsession. As with each of the other clues, of course, obsession may have a variety of meanings (e.g., anger, fascination, fear, sexual attraction), and there is no by-the-numbers guide to what it means or its implications for the therapist, the client, and the therapy.

Therapists who find that a client is constantly on their mind, who find their thoughts returning again and again to the client, who find their daydreams drifting repeatedly to the client can, if they will only attend to this clue, begin to unravel the meaning of the obsession. The most difficult part when we obsess about a client (it is much less difficult to recognize when it is someone else who is obsessing) tends to be recognizing that obsessing is a clue that something is going on that warrants attention and exploration.

Interesting Slips and Meaningful Mistakes

These can be among the most embarrassing clues because, if one occurs in the presence of other people (e.g., the client, a supervisor, colleagues at a case conference), the others can become aware of the therapist's unacknowledged uncomfortable feelings or responses to a taboo topic at the same time as or even before the therapist does. Here are some examples:

> A therapist wrote some brief notes in the chart of the previous client then opened the waiting room door for a new client's

first appointment. Surprised and a little caught off guard to see that the new client used a wheelchair, the therapist entered the waiting room, introduced himself, shook the client's hand, and asked the client to follow him into the office. The therapist walked into his office and, without thinking about what he was doing, closed the door behind him. Mortified, he apologized to the patient. Later, discussing the situation with a colleague, he described his own discomfort with people with disabilities and how his training program had never addressed the topic.

A male therapist who had been living with a woman with whom he shared a fulfilling romantic and sexual relationship for the past 5 years began work with a new patient, a gay man. The therapist scheduled 15 minutes between each therapy session so that he could return phone calls, record notes in the previous client's chart, review the chart of the next client, and make a quick trip, if need be, to the bathroom. It was halfway through his sixth session with his new client when the therapist noticed that when he had gone to the bathroom right before the current session, he had accidentally forgotten to zip up his fly. He did his best to cover his mistake during the rest of the session and was greatly relieved when the client left the office. Tending at first to dismiss the event as a simple but meaningless mistake, he found his memory returning to the event repeatedly over the next few days. Exploring his action more deeply, he identified it as a clue to some unresolved personal issues about sexual orientation. He decided to resume his own therapy to explore these issues more deeply.

A therapist, not yet aware that she was strongly attracted to a client, was using covert rehearsal, self-talk, and a variety of other cognitive-behavior techniques to help the patient gain self-confidence. Near the end of one session, the therapist was summing up, and, intending to say, "The whole point of this is that you've got to trust yourself!" but actually said, "The whole point of this is that you've got to trust your sex!" She was unaware of what she had actually said until the client, somewhat puzzled, asked her about it. Only then did she realize that there was something that she needed to talk over with her supervisor.

A senior counselor in a large mental health center was accustomed to offering coffee or tea to his clients. He was smitten by a new client. At the third meeting, he carefully prepared the client's coffee with just the right amount of sugar and cream. As they sat down to begin the counseling session, he was mortified to discover that he had given this client a coffee cup that his wife had given him, and that he used only when his wife visited him at his office. An extremely raunchy bit of sexual doggerel appeared on one side of the cup.

A therapist had met an extremely interesting person at a party the previous week and had decided that she would call the person after work for a date. At the end of a long, hard day, she made the call and was pleased when she heard the familiar voice answer the phone. But when she said the person's name, she quickly discovered that she had not dialed the right phone number. For some reason, she had unintentionally dialed the number of one of her long-term clients who was experiencing an intense erotic attraction toward the therapist. After she awkwardly terminated the phone conversation, it took her only a few minutes of reflection to discover that she was experiencing some erotic feelings for the client.

Some therapists' theoretical orientation holds that every slip or mistake during therapy has some significance. However, it is possible that a therapist's slips and mistakes are unrelated to the therapeutic process: They are simply slips and mistakes that we all make from time to time. What is important is to attend to them when they occur and to explore the extent to which they may have significance for the therapist or therapy.

Fantasies, Dreams, Daydreams, and Other Imaginings

When therapists fantasize about a patient while masturbating or engaging in sex with someone else, it is a not-too-subtle clue that it's probably time to consider how the therapist's sexual feelings may be interacting with the therapy process itself. Because these fantasies may include imaginary scenes of therapist–patient sex, they may be especially prone to evoke feelings of anxiety, guilt, embarrassment, fear of losing control (i.e., of subsequently engaging in sex with the patient), and many of the other reactions mentioned in the previous chapter. The therapist may therefore find it very difficult to acknowledge and examine the meaning of the fantasy as a potential clue to unacknowledged feelings about the patient.

National research studies[1] suggest that most therapists experience some sort of sexual fantasies about a patient, and a substantial minority have experienced such fantasies while engaging in sex with another person. One national study asked, "While engaging in sexual activity with someone other than a client, have you ever had sexual fantasies about someone who is or was a client?" More than one fourth (29%) answered that they had experienced such fantasies.[2] A national study conducted 1 year later found that almost half (46%) of the respondents reported experiencing some sexual fantasy (regardless of the occasion) about a patient on a rare basis, and an additional one fourth (26%) reported that they engaged in such fantasies more frequently.[3]

Fantasies, dreams, daydreams, and other imaginings may provide clues to a variety of difficult to acknowledge or uncomfortable issues. One therapist found herself anticipating that a certain client, whose politics she couldn't stand, would cancel sessions. Another began having nightmares about a client. He couldn't make sense of the dreams. Each seemed to have a com-

---

[1]Bernsen, A., Tabachnick, B. G., & Pope, K. S. (1994). National survey of social workers' sexual attraction to their clients: Results, implications, and comparison to psychologists. *Ethics & Behavior, 4*, 369–388; Pope, K. S. (1994). *Sexual involvement with therapists: Patient assessment, subsequent therapy, forensics.* Washington, DC: American Psychological Association; Pope, K. S., Keith-Spiegel, P. C., & Tabachnick, B. (1986). Sexual attraction to clients: The human therapist and the (sometimes) inhuman training system. *American Psychologist, 41*, 147–158 (also available at http://kspope.com); Pope, K. S., Tabachnick, B., & Keith-Spiegel, P. C. (1987). The ethics of practice: Beliefs and behaviors of psychologists as therapists. *American Psychologist, 42*, 993–1006 (also available at http://kspope.com); Pope, K. S. (2001). Sex between therapists and clients. In J. Worrell (Ed.), *Encyclopedia of women and gender: Sex* (pp. 955–962). New York: Academic Press.

[2]See Pope, Keith-Spiegel, and Tabachnick (1986) in footnote 1, this chapter.

[3]See Pope, Tabachnick, and Keith-Spiegel (1987) in footnote 1, this chapter.

pletely different setting and plot. Finally, while consulting with a colleague, the therapist came to realize that he was terrified of the patient, but was unsure why, and because he didn't know what to do about his fear (was it groundless? was he in danger? was he going crazy?), he had found it difficult to acknowledge.

Undue Special Treatment

Therapists may find that they are treating a patient in some special way that is different from the treatment offered to most if not all other patients. Obviously, the majority of therapists do this occasionally. Each patient is different, and each has unique needs and circumstances. The patient may be so frightened or insecure that he or she needs special assurance of procedures. The patient's work or child-care schedule may require special hours for therapy sessions. The therapist may try, with appropriate preparation, thoughtfulness, care, and safeguards, an innovative treatment approach not tried with other patients. But in all instances in which a therapist is somehow doing something exceptionally different or differently, it is worth reflecting on the question of whether the patient's clinical needs and "real-world" circumstances (e.g., the client's travel schedule requiring special therapy-scheduling considerations) serve as adequate justification for special treatment.

It is always possible that special treatment is a clue that the therapist is having difficulty addressing a taboo topic or some other source of uncomfortable feelings. The special treatment may reflect hard-to-acknowledge feelings of attraction or, conversely, compensatory reactions against negative feelings toward the patient. It may reflect a secret desire to please the patient (not experienced with other patients), to avoid the patient's disapproval or rejection, or an overidentification with the patient.

What forms does "special treatment" take? It differs, of course, for each therapist. Some of us, for example, may give our home phone numbers or addresses to a patient, may send holiday cards to the patient, or may engage in long, nonemergency phone conversations when we would not do these things with any other patient. We may encourage the patient to call us by our first name (while asking to be addressed as Dr. _____ by other patients), tell the patient how much we enjoy meeting with him or her (without discussing such reactions with other patients), or sit next to the patient on the couch (while customarily sitting alone in a chair while other patients sit or recline on the couch).

Isolation of the Client

Although it may be viewed as an example of the "special treatment" noted in the previous section, therapists' attempts to isolate a client—from family and friends, from other people and resources—can be an especially helpful clue to unacknowledged feelings. The isolation can serve many purposes related to therapists' sexual attraction, desires, and arousal. The isolation can make the client more dependent on the therapist, intensify the feelings that the client has for the therapist, and make it more likely that the client will think about the therapist between sessions. Isolation can also serve to allay the therapist's jealous feelings. By attempting to cut the client off from whatever romantic, sexual, or intimate relationships might occur in his or her life, the therapist eliminates all competition for the client and leaves no one for the therapist to feel jealous about. As a third example, isolation can make it less likely that the client will tell anyone—at least contemporaneously—should there be any sexually intimate words or behavior between therapist and client. Whenever therapists isolate their clients, or find themselves daydreaming about, considering, or planning isolation of clients, it is worth asking if the impulse to isolate is a clue that the therapist is experiencing unacknowledged taboo feelings about that person.

Isolation of the Therapist

The converse of isolating patients is isolating therapists. Without recognizing their taboo feelings for a patient and some of the immediate reactions to those feelings (e.g., anxiety, guilt, fear), therapists may begin moving away from their colleagues and perhaps even their friends. In some instances, therapists may be trying to reduce the "stimulus overload," to give themselves a less stressful environment in which to handle the stress of feelings that they are aware of only indirectly (perhaps through chronic fatigue, somatic complaints such as headaches or upset stomachs, or difficulty sleeping or concentrating). They may reduce the number of appointments they have with their other patients, decline to accept new patients, or fail to return any phone calls. They intuitively view colleagues as threatening or stressful rather than as potentially accepting, understanding, and helpful. (Part of the purpose of this book is to enable therapists not only to acknowledge, accept, and understand their own uncomfortable feelings and reactions but also, through exploration and discovery with others in classes, seminars, workshops, or study groups, to become more able to be genuinely supportive to others who may be struggling with and stressed or distressed by feelings and reactions.) Through self-isolation, they may be seeking to protect themselves from inquiry that might lead to discovery (by the therapist as well as by others) of the therapist's unacknowledged sexual feelings.

In other instances, therapists may be expressing through their isolative behavior a guilt of which they may be but dimly, if at all, aware. It is as if they feel that they have done something unethical by experiencing taboo, secret, or uncomfortable feelings in therapy. For example, in one national study, more than four out of every five participants indicated their belief that simply to feel sexually attracted to a patient (regardless of whether the attraction is acted on by the therapist) is per se unethical.[4] This phenomenon—feeling that sexual attraction to a patient is per se unethical—may reflect the profession's historic tendency to view sexual attraction to a patient as equivalent to or somehow inextricably bound up with therapist–patient sexual intimacy (see chap. 2). In this context, the therapists' self-isolation may express a sense of shame and guilt about supposedly unethical feelings of attraction to a patient. It is as if the therapist were punishing him- or herself through banishment or ostracism. Interestingly, even when the shame and guilt push the therapist toward isolation, he or she may still be unaware of the sexual impulses that

---

[4]See Pope, Tabachnick, and Keith-Spiegel (1987) in footnote 1, this chapter.

are evoking the shame and guilt. Therapists may use isolation to punish themselves for a variety of real and imagined errors, misdeeds, and imperfections. A therapist may, for example, feel guilty about hating a patient, about not measuring up to some myth or ideal of what a therapist should be, or about avoiding important topics that are affecting the therapy.

At the other extreme, the therapist may on some level be setting the stage for some unethical or otherwise unacceptable behavior with or toward the patient. Moving away from contact with others may seem to protect the therapist against discovery that he or she is engaging in strange or questionable patterns of conduct with a patient or is somehow acting differently. (As with many efforts to escape detection, isolation seems to call attention to the therapist and to make colleagues curious about the therapist's withdrawal. Paradoxically, it may make detection of questionable behavior more likely.) Whenever a therapist begins a process of isolation, withdrawing from customary patterns of supervision, consultation, and therapy, it may be a clue that unacknowledged taboo, secret, or uncomfortable thoughts or feelings are occurring.

Creating a Secret

One of the most salient clues that there may be taboo topics or unacknowledged feelings is the therapist's efforts to impose secrecy on the patient. Typically, of course, therapy involves privacy and confidentiality. The therapist is required, with some carefully delineated legal exceptions, to keep private what the patient reveals as part of the therapeutic process. In some instances, however, the therapist will urge or direct the patient to keep secret the contents of therapy. The therapist may rationalize this secrecy through a variety of concepts such as (a) the therapy will not "work" unless the patient keeps it in the session; (b) the patient must speak of certain "special" topics only to the therapist because only the therapist is capable of handling these issues safely; (c) other people—including other therapists—are too conventional, narrow-minded, inhibited, sexually repressed, or just downright stupid to understand the unique, advanced, revolutionary methods of the therapist; (d) no one else has the empathy and kindness that the therapist possesses and therefore no one else will be capable of accepting the patient and giving him or her the necessary understanding and support; (e) therapist and patient share a very special relationship that no one else would . . . uh . . . appreciate and understand; or (f) the patient must "save up" feelings about particular topics and "discharge" them only in therapy. Whatever the rationale, the shared sense of secrecy may enhance the feelings of intimacy between therapist and patient, may encourage them to feel "set apart" from the rest of society, and, not incidentally, may make it less likely that the patient would tell anyone else that the therapist is saying or doing something that, at best, would be highly questionable.

Whenever a therapist feels tempted to impose some sort of secrecy on the relationship with a patient, it is worthwhile to explore whether the impulse to secrecy is a clue that inadequately acknowledged feelings may exist that need to be identified, accepted, and examined. Particularly if the therapist feels that this is not a good case for consultation, this clue may suggest that consultation could be very useful.

Seeking Repeated Reassurance From Colleagues

Consultation—particularly when the consultant is someone chosen to question, explore, advise, or guide rather than merely to validate—is one of the therapist's most valuable resources. Consultation can always play an important role, but there are times when therapists are likely to rely more heavily on it: early in the career, when the newness of being a therapist can magnify feelings of insecurity; when the therapist is returning to work after a serious illness, loss, or trauma and wants additional support; and when the therapist is working with a patient who has many severe problems, with some of which the therapist may be relatively unfamiliar. Our view is that consultation is always a good idea. If a therapist is considering whether to obtain consultation, it is probably the better course to go ahead and consult. Like the judgment that one's own salary is much too high, getting too much consultation is an exceedingly rare occurrence.

In some instances, increased consultation, especially consultation of a particular type, may be a clue to unacknowledged taboo, secret, or uncomfortable thoughts or feelings. The therapist seeks repeated consultation about a patient, but the consultation sessions do not seem to move much beyond their starting point. The therapist seems to seek reassurance more than an opportunity for exploration and guidance. Each consultation session seems to take the same general form as the previous one: The same questions are asked, the same issues raised, and the same observations and reassurances given. The therapist does not have a particular question to ask as the focus for consultation but continues to struggle with a vague sense that "something isn't right."

Instances in which unacknowledged thoughts or feelings prompt repeated quests for reassurance from a consultant provide one of the most fascinating clues. Although the therapist may be unaware of the reason for seeking consultation, he or she is taking active steps that make it more likely that the taboo, secret, or uncomfortable impulses or feelings will come to awareness (with the help of the consultant). Like the interesting slips and meaningful mistakes noted in a previous section, repetitive consultation seeking about a particular patient can be potentially embarrassing because someone else (i.e., the consultant) may become aware of the therapist's reactions to a patient before the therapist gains this awareness. A sensitive, informed, and respectful consultant, however, can minimize this potential embarrassment and can help the therapist to identify, accept, and understand the uncomfortable feelings, impulses, and accompanying reactions.

Boredom and Drowsiness as Protective Reactions

The final example of a possible clue to unacknowledged feelings or issues is boredom or drowsiness with a patient. The therapist finds it hard, if not impossible, to pay attention to what a patient is saying. The patient's words seem to deflect the therapist's awareness to the physical aspects of the consulting room, to memories of the days' events, to anticipation of patients scheduled for later in the day or week, or to daydreams and fantasies that seem completely unrelated to the patient. Sometimes a patient seems to induce a drowsiness that falls over the therapist session after session after session. Each session seems interminable. The clock face is frozen. No matter how alert and engaged the therapist was during the previous patient's session or will be during the subsequent patient's session, the therapist feels drugged, comatose, daunted by the seemingly impossible tasks of concentrating and keeping his or her eyes open.

The emotional numbness associated with sustained boredom or drowsiness that recurs from session to session with a particular patient may be a clue that the therapist is on some level fighting against awareness of taboo topics or acutely uncomfortable feelings or impulses. Picking up the clue for careful examination, of course, may be difficult in light of the dulled nature of the therapist's customary alertness and by the prospect that examination will lead to direct awareness of uncomfortable feelings or impulses.

The possible clues listed in this chapter are only a few examples of those that often occur when taboo topics or uncomfortable feelings remain unacknowledged. As with the reactions discussed in the previous chapter, study groups can probably make best use of this chapter not only by using it as a basis for discussion but also by extending the list through drawing on the personal experiences and observations of the participants.

Having considered the purpose and plan of the learning experience for which this book was created (chap. 1), reviewed an example of the profession's relation to a taboo topic (chap. 2), established the conditions in which taboo topics, secrets, and uncomfortable feelings can be safely explored (chap. 3), conducted a self-assessment (chap. 4), and considered possible clues to unacknowledged topics and feelings (chap. 5), readers are now ready to explore their reactions to the passages and scenarios (chap. 6).

Before beginning that exploration, it might be useful and important for study groups to take a brief period to discuss the process of preparation they have completed through these first five chapters. If there are lingering apprehensions, doubts, or confusions about task and process, or if new apprehensions, doubts, or

confusions have arisen during the course of preparation, participants must take responsibility for giving them voice and attention. Spending a short period of time touching on each of the conditions for learning set forth in chapter 3 from this vantage point
(i.e., the group having worked together through the first five chapters and pausing before beginning chap. 6) may be particularly
meaningful.

The journey of exploration and discovery represented by chapter 6 deserves a safe and supportive learning environment, one
that meets the criteria set forth in chapter 3 and the individual
needs of each participant. Open and honest discussion of these
criteria and needs (some of which may have become apparent
during the process of working through the first five chapters)
helps form the necessary foundation of the process of exploration and discovery of the feelings that are the topic of this book. It
also facilitates the career-long process of continuing exploration
and discovery, of creating and maintaining professional commu-
nities in which such exploration and discovery are a shared venture, and of developing the trust and helpfulness we need to work
with each other as we encounter some of the most private aspects
of our experience with patients.

6

Passages and Scenarios
for Exploration

The following passages and scenarios provide an opportunity for exploring topics that tend to be taboo, receive only superficial treatment, or provoke anxiety, discomfort, and confusion. The passages offer opportunities to explore reactions to situations selected from the psychotherapy literature and to participate in a shared learning experience with colleagues. The scenarios address the reader directly and invite a more immediate, intense identification.

The most useful passages and scenarios may be those that catch us off guard or off balance, creating an unexpected or puzzling response. However much they may temporarily threaten our sense of ourselves as self-aware and centered in our knowledge of ourselves, these surprising personal reactions can help illuminate inner territory that often remains out of awareness or at least unexamined.

Chapter 1 discussed certain myths that make it hard for us to deal realistically with issues that we tend to avoid, deny, discount, distort, or treat superficially:

- ☐ Therapists learn therapy and practice in organizations free of competition's influence.
- ☐ If you're a good therapist, the money will take care of itself.
- ☐ Therapists are invulnerable, immortal, and ageless.

☐ With their extensive education and training, therapists have a firm grasp of logic and, whatever the limits of their knowledge, do not fall prey to basic logical fallacies.

☐ Learning ethical standards, principles, and guidelines, along with examples of how they have been applied, translates into ethical practice.

Chapter 2 suggested another myth: *Good* therapists never have sexual feelings about their patients, don't become sexually aroused during therapy sessions, don't vicariously enjoy the (sometimes) guilty pleasures of their patients' sexual experiences, and don't have sexual fantasies or dreams about their patients. The passages and scenarios may bring to mind these six myths or other myths that afflict our training and the services we provide.

We recommend that the first question readers address after reading a passage or scenario is this: What am I feeling? In some cases, the immediate personal response may be vague or elusive. There may be a temptation to rely on socially acceptable "stock" responses, to manage discomfort with a quick joke, or to substitute a more intellectual observation (perhaps based on theory or research) as a hedge against the immediacy and unpredictability of an idiosyncratic emotional response. Maintaining a nonjudgmental, mindful awareness of these temptations and the texture of feelings from which they arise can be an important resource for exploration, discovery, and learning.

Each passage and scenario is followed by a set of questions that may be useful in exploring these difficult topics. This set of questions is not, of course, intended to be an exhaustive list, but may provide a helpful starting point for exploration.

Beginning and Ending the Session

A new client whose life is guided by religious devotion asks if it would be OK if the two of you begin and end each session with a brief prayer.

Questions

1. What feelings are you aware of as you imagine yourself as the therapist in this scenario?

2. Do you believe that there is a "politically correct" or a "therapeutically correct" response to this client's question? If so, what is politically correct and what is therapeutically correct in these circumstances?

3. What thoughts, speculations, or hypotheses do you have about this client on the basis of this request?

4. How, if at all, do your own feelings about and experiences with religion influence how you respond to the client?

5. Under what circumstances, if any, would you agree to the client's request? Under what circumstances, if any, would you refuse the client's request?

6. Do you believe that most of your colleagues would respond to this scenario in basically the same way you would (in terms of granting or refusing the client's request)? Why or why not?

7. Would your response to the client be any different if that client asked you to pray for him or her or to "please keep me in your prayers" between therapy sessions?

8. How would you discuss this matter with your supervisor? How do you believe your supervisor would respond?

9. How would you chart this matter?

10. Does this scenario evoke any of the myths described earlier in the book or suggest any other myth to you?

Initial Appointment

In independent practice, you've been working in your new office for about a year. In the last few months, several of your patients have completed therapy, and new referrals haven't been coming in. It has become difficult to cover your expenses. Finally, a prospective patient schedules an initial appointment. During the first session, the patient says that the problem is sexual in nature and asks whether you are comfortable and experienced in working with that sort of problem. You answer truthfully that you are. You are told that the patient would only be able to work with a therapist of a particular sexual orientation, without specifying what that orientation is. Then the patient asks, "What is your sexual orientation?"

Questions

1. Imagine that the question takes you by surprise. What might you say to the patient if the question took you off guard?
2. Reflect on the various ways you might respond to this question. If you had adequate time to consider the question, how do you think you would respond? Is this response different from the one you might tend to make if the question caught you off guard?
3. Imagine that the patient has been in therapy with you for 6 months and then asks this question. Would you give a different answer than if he or she were a new patient?
4. If you were choosing a therapist, would the therapist's sexual orientation make any difference in your decision?
5. Do you believe that there are any false stereotypes about therapists based on their sexual orientation? If so, what are they? How, if at all, do they affect therapy research, theory, and training? How, if at all, do they affect hiring practices, promotions, and formal or informal policies within mental health facilities? How, if at all, have they affected your training and practice? What feelings do these false stereotypes that you believe exist evoke in you?
6. Do you believe that there are any actual group differences between therapists based on their sexual orientation? If so, what are they? How, if at all, do they affect therapy research, theory, and training? How, if at all, do they affect hiring practices, promotions, and formal or informal policies within mental health facilities? How, if at all, have they affected your training and practice? What feelings do the group differences that you believe exist evoke in you?
7. How do you decide what kinds of personal information to reveal to a patient?

The Movie

It has been an extremely demanding week, and you're looking forward to going to a new movie with your life partner. The theater is packed, but you find two seats on the aisle not too close to the screen. You feel great to have left work behind you at the office and to be with your lover for an evening on the town. As the lights go down, you lean over to give your partner a passionate kiss. For some reason, while kissing, you open your eyes and notice that, sitting in the seat on the other side of your partner, watching you, is a therapy patient who has, just that afternoon, revealed an intense sexual attraction to you.

Questions

1. If you were the therapist, what, if anything, would you say to the patient at the time of this event?
2. What would you say during the next therapy session?
3. How would the patient's presence affect your subsequent behavior at the theater?
4. How might this event affect the therapy and your relationship with the patient?
5. What, if anything, would you say to your partner, either at the theater or later, about what had happened?
6. Are there any circumstances under which you would phone the patient before the next scheduled appointment to discuss the matter?
7. Imagine that during a subsequent therapy session the patient begins asking about whom you were with at the theater. How would you feel? What would you say?
8. What if the patient were a business client of your partner (or knew your partner in another context) and they begin talking before the movie begins. What feelings would this discovery evoke in you? What would you consider in deciding how to handle this matter?
9. To what extent do you believe that therapists should be free to "be themselves"?
10. To what extent should they behave in public as if a patient might be observing them?
11. What myths, if any, does this scenario suggest to you?

The New Client

You begin psychotherapy with a new client who is extremely anxious but seems motivated. The first session focuses both on the client's intense anxiety and on finances: The client had been making quite a bit of money, but recently work has not been going so well, and it is a struggle to make ends meet. Because the client seems in crisis (although shows no evidence of being a threat to self or others), you agree to the client's request to schedule a session the next day. The second session again focuses on both anxiety and finances but also expands to discuss family issues: The client's partner is a retired attorney who no longer brings in any income, and there are three children in the home. When the client fails to show up for the third appointment, you call the contact numbers and learn from the partner that your client died from complications of a barbiturate addiction. The client had been trying to kick the habit without help and had not realized that the withdrawal was causing the anxiety. The partner yells that your assessment must have shown that the client was anxious and at risk for death because of barbiturate withdrawal and that your failure to recognize or do anything about it killed your client.

Questions

1. What are your feelings as you read this scenario, imagining yourself to be the therapist?
2. Do you believe that you've done anything wrong?
3. Do you feel at all responsible for the client's death?
4. How would you like to respond to the client's partner?
5. How do you think you would actually respond to the client's partner?
6. Would you attend the client's funeral, send flowers, or mark the funeral in any way? What do you consider as you make this decision?
7. How would you chart this?
8. Would this incident influence you to change your procedures in any way? If so, how?
9. Would you be concerned about the possibility of a malpractice suit or licensing complaint? If so, is there anything you would do to try to minimize the possibility of a suit or complaint?
10. Are you afraid, anxious, or concerned that you might miss something or make a mistake in therapy that might lead,

or seem to lead, to a client's death? If so, how do you handle these feelings? With whom do you discuss them? Are the discussions helpful?

The Therapist's Fear of Showing Feeling: A Passage From Clara Thompson

Clara Thompson, one of the "neo-Freudians," traced the intricate patterns of influence and change in analytic theory and practice in her book *Psychoanalysis: Its Evolution and Development*.[1] In the following passage, she described the conflicts among analysts in the 1920s regarding whether the analyst must maintain the "blank screen" with patients or become more active, even adopting feelings of friendliness toward the patients.

> Freud always knew that it was sometimes not possible for the analyst to remain entirely out of the picture, that sometimes, in spite of everything, he would react personally to the patient and what he said or did. This he saw as counter-transference, by which he meant that analysts sometimes transfer elements from their past (or present) problems to the analytic situation. Thus one might be susceptible to the flattery of a patient's erotic interest or one might be hurt by a hostile attack on a vulnerable spot. Because of the stress on the unfortunate aspects of the analyst's involvement, the feeling grew that even a genuine objective feeling of friendliness on his part was to be suspected. As a result, many of Freud's pupils became afraid to be simply human and show the ordinary friendliness and interest a therapist customarily feels for a patient. In many cases, out of fear of showing counter-transference, the attitude of the analyst became stilted and unnatural. (p. 107)

Questions

1. Does being a professional seem somehow at odds with being human or showing friendliness toward a patient?
2. Have you ever regretted your spontaneity with a patient? What do you think may have occurred?

---

[1]Thompson, C. (1950). *Psychoanalysis: Its evolution and development*. New York: Hermitage House.

3. Does this passage remind you of any myths about therapists?
4. Do you think that any of your patients perceive you as stilted and unnatural? Is there any truth to their perception? Is there any aspect of your professional appearance or style that seems awkward or artificial?
5. If they were interviewed and gave completely honest responses, what words do you think your patients might use to describe you and your manner?
6. What words do you think your patients might use to describe how they feel about you and your manner?
7. If they were interviewed and gave completely honest responses, what words do you think your supervisors might use to describe you and your manner?
8. What words do you think your supervisors might use to describe how they feel about you and your manner?

The Perfect Therapist

During the first two sessions, a new client focuses on feelings of rage, which seem to alternate with plunges into profound depression. At the start of the third session, the client says,

> I am so happy I found you. You come so highly recommended, and I think you really understand what I'm going through. You seem just perfect for me. You know, I almost gave up. The first therapist I wound up with, I liked him at first but he mistreated me horribly! He should lose his license! I've filed a complaint with the licensing board. And I'm looking for a new attorney to handle a suit against him. I'd thought I had an attorney I could trust, but he made all sorts of mistakes and just tried to steal my money, so I filed a complaint with the state bar. But to get back to what we were talking about last week. . . .

Questions

1. As you read this scenario, imagining that you were the therapist, what feelings did you experience when the client said, "I am so happy I found you. You come so highly

recommended, and I think you really understand what I'm going through. You seem just perfect for me."?

2. How, if at all, did your feelings change when the client began talking about the prior therapist?

3. How, if at all, did your feelings change when the client began talking about filing a complaint against the prior therapist and the attorney?

4. What concerns, if any, would you have about your work with this client on the basis of this statement?

5. To what degree do you want clients to like you, to believe you are a good (why not "outstanding"?) therapist, and to express their positive feelings to you? If so, have you ever discussed these feelings with a supervisor? Why or why not?

6. Has a client ever idealized you—that is, viewed you in a positive way that was not realistic? If so, how did you feel and how did you respond?

Cognitive–Behavioral Approach to "Ugly": A Passage From Ellen Toby Klass and Joann Paley Galst

In her fascinating book, *Women as Therapists, A Multitheoretical Casebook*, Dorothy Cantor[2] asked a therapist to present a case study and then invited therapists from different theoretical orientations to describe how they might have handled the treatment. The case study in the following passage was presented by Karen Zager.[3] It concerned a young man who felt "depressed, ugly, and bad" (p. 145).

Ellen Toby Klass and Joann Paley Galst[4] described a cognitive–behavioral approach to treating the young man. For stylistic convenience, Klass and Galst used the first person singular

[2]Cantor, D. W. (1990). *Women as therapists: A multitheoretical casebook*. Northvale, NJ: Jason Aronson.

[3]Zager, K. (1990). The case. In D. W. Cantor (Ed.), *Women as therapists: A multitheoretical casebook* (pp. 145–152). Northvale, NJ: Jason Aronson.

[4]Klass, E. T., & Galst, J. P. (1990). A cognitive–behaviorist views the case. In D. W. Cantor (Ed.), *Women as therapists: A multitheoretical casebook* (pp. 198–274). Northvale, NJ: Jason Aronson.

(i.e., "I"). In addressing how they would work with the patient around his feelings of ugliness, they draw on cognitive–behavioral techniques developed to foster among women greater self-acceptance of their bodies and images of their bodies. They described an approach that provides a sympathetic invitation for the client to put words to his deep feelings about himself and his appearance.

> This experience would provide exposure to avoided content (on the rationale of allowing extinction of conditioned emotional reactions), and the emotionality might also facilitate needed change. I would then ask [the patient] how he learned to feel so ugly and would trace the feelings associated with specific incidents. Since [the patient] was so unquestioning about his unattractiveness, I would hope that this emotional and historical framework could help him truly entertain the idea that these self-evaluations were learned rather than necessarily factually correct. I would suggest that as a child and teenager, [the patient] had little choice but to think his peers were right. "As an adult, you may be able to learn other ways to feel about your attractiveness, hard as it is to believe that right now.". . . I would suggest that doing body mirror exercise at home might be very interesting, and I would help him devise tolerable hierarchical steps to do so. I would also try to broaden [the patient's] view of the basis for attractiveness. (pp. 215–216)

Questions

1. When a client discusses body image, what feelings does it evoke in you? To what extent do such factors as the client's age, gender, race, sexual orientation, cultural background, and socioeconomic status influence your feelings?
2. When a client talks about feeling ugly and unattractive, what feelings are evoked in you?
3. Have you ever found yourself comparing your client's attractiveness to your own?
4. Have you ever envied a client's attractiveness?
5. Have you ever resented a client's attractiveness?
6. Have you ever been repelled because you experienced a client as extremely unattractive?

7. Have you ever felt pity for a client because you perceived him or her to be extremely unattractive?

8. What events or factors have been most influential in shaping your sense of your own attractiveness?

9. What role do our society's predominant standards of physical attractiveness play in your assessment and treatment of clients?

10. How do you feel when working with clients who are hyperobese or extremely emaciated?

11. Imagine that you are working with two clients who are reasonably matched for all factors except an aspect of attractiveness. Both clients are distressed because they think that they are extremely ugly, that no one would find them attractive. The only difference between the two is this: You believe that one of them is one of the most beautiful people you have ever encountered; you believe that the other is one of the most unattractive people you have encountered. Do you use the same therapeutic approach with both clients? Or does your personal appraisal of their attractiveness influence you to use different therapeutic interventions? What if each client were to ask you if you found him or her attractive? How would you feel? How would you respond?

12. When writing notes about clients regarding an intake screening, a mental status examination, a psychological assessment, or a course of therapy, to what extent do you mention client attractiveness? If you reviewed all of your charts, would attractiveness be mentioned in equal proportions of your male clients' and your female clients' charts?

The Two-Person Practice

For the past 12 years, you and a colleague have shared a two-person psychology practice: Each of you schedules about 30 hours of therapy a week and devotes the rest of the time to paper work, marketing the practice, and other details necessary to keep the practice going. You split all expenses and all income down the middle. On a day when each of you has a full schedule of clients, you arrive at the office and notice that your colleague has not yet arrived and that your colleague's first client of the day has been waiting for 35 minutes. You call your colleague's home and find out from your colleague's partner that your colleague committed suicide the night before. There is no professional will or instructions, your colleague's charts are locked in a filing cabinet to which you do not have the key, and your first client of the day has just shown up.

Questions

1. What feelings did you experience as you read this scenario?
2. What would you like to do if you were in such a situation?
3. What do you think you actually would do in such a situation?
4. To what degree do you believe that therapists and therapists-in-training are encouraged and supported in monitoring their own mental health in regard to depression and other factors that, if not adequately addressed, might affect their ability to practice competently?
5. What factors or myths, if any, do you believe might make therapists and therapists-in-training reluctant to acknowledge (to themselves or to others) their own psychological problems?
6. To what degree have you made an adequate professional will and made other arrangements should you become suddenly unable to practice? If you have made a professional will, what does it contain and who has copies of it?

The Request

You have been working with a client for about a year and believe that things are going well. Suddenly the client stops coming to sessions and does not respond to any of your messages. You receive a call from the client's attorney who requests the client's chart and asks that any future communications be not to the client but to the attorney. When you ask if the client intends to sue, the attorney declines to answer but comments that if you have any concerns it would be a good idea for you to discuss them with an attorney. The attorney then asks how much professional liability coverage you have.

Questions

1. What feelings did you experience as you read this scenario, imagining yourself to be the therapist?
2. What concerns would you have under these circumstances, and how would you respond to those concerns?
3. Would you send the chart to the attorney, and, if so, what steps, if any, would you take before sending it?
4. In what ways, if at all, do you believe that concerns about the possibility of a lawsuit have influenced your education and training, your development as a therapist, and the ways that you practice? Currently, how realistic (rather than understated, overstated, or otherwise distorted) do each of these concerns seem to you? If you believe that concerns about lawsuits have been influential, to what degree do you believe that the influences have been positive, and to what degree negative?

Telling a Client to Undress During a Therapy Session: A Passage From Milton Erickson

Milton Erickson, who died in 1980, was an extremely active hypnotist, hypnotizing more than 30,000 people.[5] Training at the University of Wisconsin and Colorado General Hospital, he received a doctorate in medicine and a master's degree in psychology. Founding president of the American Society for Clinical Hypnosis, he was a fellow of both the American Psychological Association and the American Psychiatric Association.

Haley[6] described Erickson's hypnotic techniques as a form of strategic therapy. "Therapy can be called strategic if the clinician initiates what happens during therapy and designs a particular approach for each problem" (p. 1). To accomplish profound change in one or only a few sessions, Erickson used a variety of techniques such as fostering resistance, pointing out negative options, and creatively using metaphors.

---

[5]Williams, J. (1980, March 29). Milton H. Erickson, hypnosis authority. *New York Times*, p. 28.

[6]Haley, J. (1973). *Uncommon therapy: The psychiatric techniques of Milton H. Erickson*. New York: Ballantine Books.

Erickson described the following intervention in 1959 during a conversation with Jay Haley and John Weakland. A young woman had become engaged, but kept putting off the engagement. She was afraid of marriage and began to develop phobias. Erickson's first intervention was to direct that the woman move out of her mother's house. "I made her move. A Spanish family. The grandmother . . . laid down the law . . ., but I had laid down the law first"[7] (p. 127).

After working with her about her travel phobias, Erickson turned to the issue of sex. Every time the topic came up, the woman acted as if she could not communicate in any way. To address this issue, Erickson told her that she must bring to the next session the most abbreviated pair of shorts she could find. At the next session, he told her to show him the shorts. As they looked at the shorts, he posed a dilemma for her: She must either come to the next session dressed in those shorts, or he would make her put them on in the consulting room.

The woman arrived at the next session wearing the shorts. Then Erickson posed another dilemma: She must either pay attention as he addressed the sexual issues that were troubling her or he would direct her to remove the shorts and put them back on while she was with him. She began to pay attention as he began to talk about the sexual issues that had been plaguing her.

During a subsequent session, he directed her to confront her sexual fears in a way that was both direct and symbolic.

> I said, "Now you need to know how to undress and go to bed in the presence of a man. So start undressing." Slowly, in an almost automatic fashion, she undressed. I had her show me her right breast, her left breast, her right nipple, her left nipple. Her belly button. Her genital area. Her knees. Her gluteal regions. I asked her to point where she would like to have her husband kiss her. I had her turn around slowly. She dressed. I dismissed her. (p. 128)[8]

Erickson reports that she was then able to travel freely (i.e., without the debilitating phobias), to make the wedding arrange-

---

[7]Haley, J. (Ed.). (1985). *Conversations with Milton H. Erickson: Vol. 2. Changing couples.* New York: Norton (Triangle Press).
[8]See footnote 7, this chapter.

ments, and to have a happy marriage including children. He also reports that she wrote him later to express her gratitude for the help he had given to her.

In addressing the question of why the client followed his directions, Erickson explains that the key is the therapist's expectations that the patient will follow the instructions. The patient comes to understand that the therapist knows that the therapeutic behavior is absolutely essential. He draws a connection to an influential lesson he learned as an intern from a professor at the Colorado School of Medicine. The professor stressed that in some cases

> the only way you can get a woman to consent to have an amputation of the breast for cancer . . . is by stripping her to the nude and doing a very careful medical examination . . . with your eyes . . . and then you tell her, "I'm very, very positive you need the amputation . . . I'm awfully sorry." . . . You can get some women, who would otherwise go to the grave, to enter the operating room gladly, hopefully. (pp. 128–129)[9]

Questions

1. Erickson mentions that the woman comes from a Spanish family. What influence, if any, does this have on your understanding of and reaction to the events described in this passage?
2. What difference would it make (in your understanding of and reaction to the events) if the therapist were female? Why?
3. What difference would it make if the patient were male? Why?
4. Would it make any difference whether the therapist is a medical doctor?
5. Would the age of the therapist or patient (e.g., very young, middle-aged, very old) make any difference in the way you react to or understand the events described in this passage?
6. Would the race or ethnicity of the therapist or patient make any difference in the way you react to or understand the events described in this passage?

[9]See footnote 7, this chapter.

7. Imagine that you seek therapy for difficulties similar to those experienced by the woman in this passage and that your therapist uses a similar approach. How would you react?

8. Do you believe such interventions might increase the likelihood of a positive outcome or might shorten the course of therapy? To what extent does your belief about efficacy or efficiency influence your decisions about learning and using such interventions?

9. Under what circumstances would you "lay down the law" to a patient? How do you feel about giving commands to a patient?

10. Have you had any experiences with professors or supervisors in which their treatment philosophy profoundly influenced your own approach? How did you evaluate the validity of their views? In the most memorable instance of such influence, how did the professor or supervisor "teach" you (e.g., lecture, dialogue, demonstration, modeling, giving you directions about what to do)?

Staffing Patterns

You are executive director of a large clinic but also do clinical work. During a session of group therapy, one of the patients says, "You know, there's something I've always wondered about. Virtually all of the professional staff at your clinic are White, and virtually all the janitorial staff are racial minorities. How do you think that affects us patients, and why did you set up your clinic that way?" The group members look to you, eager to hear your response.

Questions

1. How did you feel as you read this scenario?
2. What issues, if any, would you consider before responding to the patient's question?
3. How do you believe you would respond to the patient's question?
4. What do you imagine might be the reaction to your response?

5. As you imagined this scenario, what was the racial composition of the group? How, if at all, would the racial makeup of the therapy group affect your response to the question?

6. Have you ever seen a clinic or other facility with staffing patterns similar to those described in this scenario? If so, how, if at all, did the staffing patterns affect you? Did the staffing patterns evoke any thoughts or feelings in you?

7. In what ways, if at all, has race played a role in your education and training as a therapist?

8. To what extent have issues of race been openly and honestly discussed in the facilities you're familiar with that provide education, training, or services? In any of those facilities, have there been any taboos about race?

9. Are there any topics about race that make you uncomfortable in any way?

10. Have you ever been struck by other staffing patterns in terms of gender or other characteristics?

11. Does this scenario evoke any of the myths described in chapter 1 or suggest any other myths to you?

A Client's Anger at a Therapist's Voyeurism: A Passage From Laura Brown

In an article discussing the negative consequences of posttermination sexual relationships involving lesbians, Laura Brown[10] emphasized an interesting point: When a client learns that her (or his) therapist has been sexually intimate with another client, either before or after termination, the client may begin to wonder about the therapist's reactions to sexual issues in therapy.

> To quote one former client of such a therapist, "The thought that she's been sitting around getting her jollies by listening to my sexual experiences and concerns enrages me!" These clients consistently espouse the view that the relationship, although genitally sexual only in posttermination, must have begun its sexual and romantic component in therapy; this overt

---

[10]Brown, L. (1988). Harmful effects of posttermination sexual and romantic relationships with former clients. *Psychotherapy, 25,* 249–255.

revelation of the countertransferential aspect of the psychotherapy process is distinctly unsettling even to sophisticated clients and former clients who are themselves therapists. The fear that a therapist will not protect them from their own regressed or transferential feelings can be overwhelming, and may serve as a barrier to seeking out therapy for fear of encountering it in another therapist. (p. 253)

Questions

1. Do you enjoy hearing about the sexual activities of some patients more than others? What influences your reactions?
2. Have you ever found yourself asking for more details about a sexual encounter than was probably necessary for your work?
3. Do you ever feel like asking a patient not to talk about his or her body or sexuality? Why?
4. Have you ever sensed that a client was trying (consciously or unconsciously) to arouse you sexually? What feelings did the client's behavior evoke in you? Did you become aroused either at the time or later when recollecting the experience? What influenced you to disclose or not to disclose to the client your interpretation of the purpose of the behavior?
5. Is there any kind of sexual behavior that you consider very strange or bizarre? How would you feel if a patient revealed this kind of sexual behavior to you? How would it affect communication between you and the patient?

The Requirement

A new client shows up for the first session and begins by saying,

> I have a request that may be unusual, but it will tell me whether we can work together or not. I work in an extremely sensitive job requiring government clearance. There are some other factors that I can't mention right now. But I need the fact that I am in therapy and the content of what I want to discuss to remain absolutely confidential, and therefore I want no records of our meetings to be made at all. I want your word that you will never write down any contact information for me—the

name I gave your receptionist in setting up this appointment was a pseudonym —no records of payment, no records of when we meet, and nothing about what we discuss. I will pay for each session in cash at the beginning of the session. I know that some therapists say that records are safe because they are kept in a safe to which only the therapist has the key, or do not have the client's name on them, or are kept in encrypted form. I know that mistakes can happen with each of those and that there are ways around them. If you're willing to assure me that there will be no documentation of our work, let's begin now. If not, I'll pay you for this session now and leave.

Questions

1. How did you feel as you read this scenario, imagining yourself as the therapist?
2. To what degree do you believe that the client's requirement is reasonable?
3. To what extent do you believe that the client's statements (e.g., about a sensitive job requiring government clearance) are completely accurate? If you have any doubts, how do you respond to those doubts?
4. Under what conditions, if any, would you agree to the client's requirement? Under what conditions, if any, would you refuse to agree to the client's requirement?
5. To what extent do you believe that the information you keep about clients (beginning with name and phone number) is completely safe from accidental or other (e.g., theft) forms of unauthorized disclosure?
6. Are you aware of any instances in which a therapy patient's identity, address, diagnosis, and so on have been disclosed to a third party who had no right to the information? Have you ever learned such information from another therapist because the therapist talked with the patient (e.g., on the phone) in your presence, left a chart out where you could see it, or through some other means?

Sounds

You are working in a busy mental health center in which the doors to the consulting rooms, while offering some privacy, are not completely sound-proofed. As long as therapist and client are talking at a normal level, nothing can be heard from outside the door. But words spoken loudly can be heard and understood in the reception area.

A patient, Sal, sits in silence during the first 5 minutes of the session, finally saying, "It's been hard to concentrate today. I keep hearing these sounds, like they're ringing in my ear, and they're frightening to me. I want to tell you what they're like, but I'm afraid to." After offering considerable reassurance that describing the sounds would be OK and that you and Sal can work together to try to understand what is causing the sounds, what they mean, and what you might do about them, you notice that Sal seems to be gathering the courage to reveal them to you. Finally, Sal leans back in the chair and imitates the sounds. They build quickly to a very high pitch and loud volume. They sound exactly like someone becoming more and more sexually aroused and then experiencing an intense orgasm. You are reasonably certain that these sounds have been heard by the receptionist, some of your colleagues, the patients sitting in the waiting room, and a site visitor from the Joint Commission for the Accreditation of Hospitals who is deciding whether the hospital in which your clinic is based should have its accreditation renewed.

Questions

1. As you imagined the scene, was the client male (e.g., Salvador) or female (e.g., Sally)? Does the client's gender make any difference in the way you feel?

2. If Sal began to make the sounds again, would you make any effort to interrupt or to ask the client to be a little quieter? Why?

3. If none of the people who might have heard the sounds mentioned this event to you, would you make any effort to explain what had happened?

4. Imagine that just as Sal finishes making these sounds, someone knocks loudly on the door and asks, "What's going on in there?" What do you say or do?

5. Would your feelings or behavior be any different if the sounds were of a person being beaten rather than having an orgasm?

6. How would you describe this session in your chart notes?
7. If you were being supervised, would you feel at all apprehensive about discussing this session with your supervisor?
8. What approach do you usually take toward your clients making loud noises that might be heard outside the consulting room?
9. Have you ever had a client whom you wished no one knew you were seeing—not your receptionist, your supervisor, or anyone? What led to your wish?
10. Has anything ever happened in a therapy session that you *really* did not want anyone to know about? What was it, and why did you not want others to know about it?

Are Beliefs About Race and Sex Related? A Passage From Leon Williams

Leon Williams[11] began his analysis by quoting Herndon's conclusion "that all race relations [in the United States] tend to be, however subtle, sex relations" (p. 7).[12]

Racism like sexuality is learned behavior, and on a given plane, such as America's peculiar history of slavery, "Jim Crowism" and Victorian morality, that initial, fleeting insight into the sexuality of racism, strikes us with greater clarity.

Herndon conceptualized this relationship best by calling the tangled myths of sexuality and racism the "sexualization of racism," a uniquely American phenomenon. He saw racism and sex in tandem, concluding that the two were inextricably connected.

If this, then, is the case, we must explore racism and its sexual dimension as an additional factor which may serve as a powerful constraint on the [therapist's] judgment and skill as [the therapist] attempts to practice across racial lines. . . .

---

[11]Williams, L. F. (1972). *Sex, racism, and social work*. In H. L. Gochros & L. G. Schultz (Eds.), *Human sexuality and social work* (pp. 75–81). New York: Association Press.

[12]Herndon, C. C. (1965). *Sex and racism in America*. New York: Grove Press.

Treating the two notions [race and sex] together is virtually unheard of, suggesting that powerful emotions and deeply unconscious factors have come into play to "cool out" our efforts to look critically and objectively at a subject which appears to lie at the root of social reality in America. (pp. 76, 80)

Questions

1. Are you more or less likely to become sexually aroused by a patient whose race is different from your own?
2. Are you more or less likely to touch a patient whose race is different from your own?
3. If a patient of a different race said that he or she were in love with you (or were having sexual fantasies about you), how would you feel? What would you say or do?
4. When you think about a patient of a different race, what is the first race that comes to mind? Why?
5. Is there any race for which you cannot imagine yourself making love with or being a life partner of a person of that race? If so, what influence might your propensities have on your therapy with people of that race?
6. How would you respond if a patient commented that you were racist? How would you respond if a supervisor commented that some of your views, assessments, or interventions were racist?
7. Do you believe that race is generally an important factor or generally not an important factor in therapy? Why?
8. Imagine that you begin work with a patient who expresses views and engages in behaviors that you consider to reflect racism. How do you feel? How, if at all, does this perceived racism affect your relationship with the patient and your interventions?
9. How comfortable are you discussing racial issues in supervision and case conferences? Do you discuss racial issues in supervision and case conferences?

A Request for Help

During a hospital visit with a therapy client who is in the final stages of a terminal disease, you learn that the medical team has not been able to control the client's pain. The client, who does not have the use of arms or legs, tells you of the painful agony suffered each second, and begs you to help him or her end this horror. Sobbing, the client says, "I have no friends or family who can help me with this. You're the only one I can turn to. Please help me." Each time you go to the hospital, this is what the client asks you to do.

Questions

1. How did you feel as you read this scenario, imagining yourself to be the therapist?
2. What would you consider in deciding how to respond?
3. Would you consult anyone? If so, whom?
4. Under what circumstances, if any, would you agree to the client's request? If you did agree, what would you say and do?
5. Under what circumstances, if any, would you refuse the client's request? If you refused the request, what would you say and do?
6. How would you chart the client's request?
7. How would you chart your response to the client's request?
8. Can you imagine yourself in a situation similar to that of the client in this scenario? If so, how would you like the therapist to respond to you?

The Media and the Message

You communicate with some of your clients via e-mail. You receive an emergency e-mail from a client who is well known in the community. The client has discovered that his or her partner is having an affair. The affair is with someone quite famous. The client is not in immediate danger but is beginning to experience suicidal thoughts. The client is at home that day and asks that you reply via e-mail so that the partner will not overhear any of the conversation. The client also asks that you send a copy of a document that the two of you had worked on during a therapy session—a set of specific steps that the client could take (e.g., various friends the client could contact for support) when experiencing suicidal thoughts. You find a copy of the document in electronic form and send it, along with your detailed response, to the client. A few minutes later, still at work at the computer, you notice that you accidentally misaddressed the message intended for your client, sending it by mistake to another client.

Questions

1. How did you feel as you read this scenario?
2. What would you do in regard to the client to whom you intended to send this material?
3. What would you do in regard to the client to whom you actually sent the message?
4. How would you record this incident in the chart of the client to whom you intended to send the message?
5. How would you record this incident in the chart of the client to whom you actually sent the message?
6. How, if at all, would you change your procedures?
7. Have you ever accidentally sent an e-mail message to the wrong address?
8. Are you aware of any instances in which others have sent sensitive messages to the wrong address?

Beatings, Grief, Love, and Sex: A Passage From Fritz Perls

Fritz Perls (1893–1970) was one of the founders of Gestalt therapy. As accounts of his life and work describe,[13] he practiced psychoanalysis in Berlin until the Nazi movement forced his emigration. He was analyzed by Wilhelm Reich; was supervised by Helene Deutsch, Otto Fenichel, and Karen Horney; and worked for a brief period as an assistant to Kurt Goldstein. In the 1930s, Perls moved

---

[13]Perls, F. S. (1969). *In and out of the garbage pail*. New York: Bantam; Perls, F. S. (1973). *The Gestalt approach & eye witness to therapy*. New York: Science and Behavior Books; Perls, F. S. (1988). *Gestalt therapy verbatim*. Highland, NY: Center for Gestalt Development. (Original work published 1969); Shepard, M. (1976). *Fritz*. New York: Bantam.

to South Africa, where he founded the South African Institute of Psychoanalysis.

Later moving to Miami, he found that his marriage was no longer fulfilling, and he began engaging, according to his own account, in affairs that were unaccompanied by any deep emotional attachment. Soon, however, he met a woman to whom he wrote an open letter in his autobiography, addressing her as "the most important person in my life" (p. 196).[14] According to Shepard,[15] she had been attending individual therapy sessions with Perls for 3 to 5 days each week. Shepard quoted her description of the turning point in therapy. Perls had been giving her friendly, supportive kisses at the end of each session. At the end of one session, the kiss became erotic. According to Shepard, she told him, "I need a therapist, not a lover" (p. 81).[16] She then had a dream, which she described during a subsequent session. It was after she reviewed the dream that she, according to Shepard's account, decided to become Perls's lover.

Once he had arrived in the United States, Perls began to devote more time and energy to the development of Gestalt therapy. In the early 1950s, he founded the New York Institute for Gestalt Therapy and the Cleveland Institute for Gestalt Therapy. In the 1960s, he found a community that felt like "home" to him: the Esalen Institute in Big Sur, California.

Perls viewed Gestalt therapy as an existential approach that dealt with the whole person. "The difference between Gestalt Therapy and most other types of psychotherapy is essentially that we do not analyze. We integrate" (pp. 65–66).[17] The integration took place in and focused on the present. "Psychotherapy then becomes not an excavation of the past, in terms of repressions, Oedipal conflicts, and primal scenes, but an experience in living in the present" (p. 15).[18]

In the following passage, Perls recounts his intervention with a woman in a group at Esalen. The woman had begun physically

---

[14]See Perles (1969) in footnote 13, this chapter.
[15]See Shepard (1976) in footnote 13, this chapter.
[16]See Shepard (1976) in footnote 13, this chapter.
[17]See Perls (1988) in footnote 13, this chapter.
[18]See Perls (1973) in footnote 13, this chapter.

fighting with members of the group. Unable to restrain her, the group called on Perls to help bring peace.

> When I came in she charged with her head down into my belly and nearly knocked me over. Then I let her have it until I had her down on the floor. Up she came again. And then a third time. I got her down again and said, gasping: "I've beaten up more than one bitch in my life." Then she got up, threw her arms around me: "Fritz, I love you." Apparently she finally got what, all her life, she was asking for.
>
> And there are thousands of woman like her in the States. Provoking and tantalizing, bitching, irritating their husbands and never getting their spanking. You don't have to be a Parisian prostitute to need that so to respect your man. A Polish saying is: "My husband lost interest in me, he never beats me any more."(p. 98)[19]

One of the many fascinating aspects of this account is the sudden shift in the woman's feelings toward Perls. In his Gestalt approach, he was exceptionally aware of such quick emotional transformations as they occurred not only for others but also for him, as the following passage illustrates:

> And if I comfort a girl in grief or distress and the sobbing subsides and she presses closer and the stroking gets out of rhythm and slides over the hips and over the breasts . . . where does the grief end and a perfume begin to turn your nostrils from dripping to smelling? (p. 100)[20]

Questions

1. Can you imagine yourself doing the following to a patient in an attempt to teach the person how to "be open" and "stay tuned" to the present moment?
   □ pinning the person down on the floor
   □ holding the person in your lap
   □ tying the person's hands together
   □ muffling the person's face with a pillow
   □ "fighting" using big, heavy, cloth bats
2. As you imagine these scenes, how do you feel?
3. Are the feelings any different when you change the gender, race, sexual orientation, social status, or age of the imaginary patient?

---

[19]See Perls (1969) in footnote 13, this chapter.
[20]See Perls (1969) in footnote 13, this chapter.

4. How might such interventions affect someone experiencing one of the following conditions?
   - ☐ depression
   - ☐ problems with being assertive
   - ☐ posttraumatic stress syndrome
   - ☐ schizophrenia
   - ☐ panic disorder
5. How do you decide which limits to set for your own behavior during therapy? How do you decide whether to use "street language"?

What You Enjoy

You are working with a patient who is terrified of sex. Even thinking about sexual behaviors tends to make him or her feel guilty, anxious, and uncomfortable. You discuss this patient with your supervisor and note the progress that the patient is making in discussing more openly the few sexual activities that he or she enjoys. Your supervisor asks you what kind of sexual activities you enjoy.

Questions

1. How would you like to respond in this situation? Why?
2. How do you believe you actually would respond in this situation? Why?
3. How would your feelings and behaviors vary, if at all, according to factors such as the supervisor's age, gender, race, or professional status and influence?
4. How would your feelings and behaviors vary, if at all, according to whether you were sexually attracted to your supervisor?
5. Does this scenario suggest any of the myths described in chapter 1 or any other myths?

A Client in Crisis

You send out bills on the first day of each month. A new client who is in crisis begins seeing you twice a week. During the second week, in addition to the two sessions of therapy, you also conduct a 90-minute assessment session of psychological testing.

At the beginning of the next month, you send a bill for the eight therapy sessions and 90-minute testing session, but the client simply quits coming to the therapy, does not respond to your attempts at contact, and does not pay the bill. Several weeks later, on a Friday afternoon just as you are leaving the office for the weekend, you receive a fax from a well-known clinic. The fax includes a copy of a signed authorization from the patient for release of records. The client, in crisis, has been hospitalized for 72 hours of observation and evaluation regarding suicidal risk. Your records of evaluation and treatment are urgently needed so that the clinic can review the prior records as part of its emergency assessment and intervention. You are asked to fax the records immediately. If they are too extensive to fax, a clinic volunteer can pick up a copy at your office later that day (or can pick up the originals, make a copy, and return the originals).

Questions

1. How did you feel as you read this scenario?
2. What would you like to do in this situation?
3. What do you think you actually would do in this situation?
4. In what way, if at all, would your feelings influence how you would respond to this request?
5. To what extent do you or the setting where you work have clear policies and procedures for handling these matters?
6. To what extent are you aware of the current legal and ethical standards for responding to such requests?
7. To what degree do you feel adequately prepared to deal with such situations?

A Patient's Difficulties Talking About Sexual Fantasies: A Passage From Mardi Horowitz

Serving as director for the Center for the Study of Neuroses (a National Institutes of Mental Health Clinical Research Center) at the Langley Porter Institute in San Francisco, Mardi Horowitz[21]

---

[21]Horowitz, M. J. (1978). *Image formation and cognition* (2nd ed.). New York: Appleton-Century-Crofts.

conducted extensive research into how people encode their experience in three modes of representation: (a) bodily or kinesthetic, (b) imagistic, and (c) linguistic. One focus of his research is the way in which therapy can help a patient to translate material from one mode to another. In the following passage, he described a patient's difficulties talking in therapy about the visual images she experiences during intercourse with her husband.

A young married woman was sometimes sexually frigid. At other times she was able to achieve an orgasm during intercourse with her husband. Her only route to sufficient erotic excitation for orgasm was to have a specific visual fantasy during love making. In this fantasy she pictured herself as a prostitute permitting humiliating acts to be performed upon her for money. She felt guilty and tried to avoid recall of these fantasies or acknowledgment of their implications. She also feared revealing the images to the therapist because she was ashamed of them and feared that they might be regarded as abnormal. Also, translation of the images into words would destroy the compartmentalization of her mental life: she would have to recognize the images and their implications, and that meant that she might have to give up her only current route to sexual pleasure. (pp. 120–121)

Questions

1. Are there any aspects of your own sexuality about which you feel guilty or ashamed? Have you experienced any visual sexual images that you would be reluctant to translate into words? How does your own sexuality influence your reactions to this woman?
2. If you were the therapist, how would you conceptualize the patient's difficulty revealing her sexual images to you? What other possibilities are there besides the explanation set forth in the passage?
3. If you were the therapist, would you attempt to help the woman translate her sexual images into words? If so, how would you proceed? If not, how would you approach the issue?
4. Can you imagine yourself, as therapist, becoming excited or aroused as a patient describes the sexual images in the

passage or any other sexual images he or she might experience? Do you believe your excitement or arousal would increase or decrease if, instead of translating the images into words, the patient were to bring in or draw pictures of them?

The New Client

A new client who was referred to you calls you on a cell phone 10 minutes before the first appointment saying, "I'm outside your building right now but I can't get in. I use a wheelchair and your office is not accessible."

Questions

1. What feelings did you experience as you read this scenario, imagining yourself as the therapist?
2. What would you say to the client?
3. What would you do?
4. How would you chart this incident?
5. To what extent, if at all, do you believe that therapists are obligated to ensure that their offices are accessible to people with disabilities?
6. Does this scenario bring to mind any of the myths described in chapter 1 or any other myths?

The Surprise Date

Just as you are about to head out for your 2-hour lunch break, your life partner surprises you by showing up, taking you to a fancy hotel, ordering room service, and sharing with you an unexpected but delightful romantic interlude, finally dropping you off at your office just in time for your next patient who is waiting for you in the reception area. You and your patient enter your office and sit down. Your face is still flushed from your sexual encounter. Your patient says, "You look like you're blushing. What's going on?"

Questions

1. If the client's question caught you off guard and you answered immediately, what do you imagine that you would say?
2. Would you answer the client's question directly? Why or why not?
3. Under what conditions might you invent a reason for your blushing to answer the client's question? How do you believe that telling the client something that is not strictly true might influence the therapy and your relationship with the client? Have you ever told a client something that you knew was false or misleading? Why? Have you ever told a supervisor something that you knew was false or misleading? Why?
4. If, on your way back into the office, a colleague rather than a client would have asked the same question, would your response have been different? If so, why?
5. To what extent do you believe that each of the clients with whom you work acknowledges that you have a private life away from work and your sessions with him or her? To what extent is each client curious about your life? What fantasies do you think your clients have about your life? Do their fantasies include your sexual behavior? To what extent do your clients' concerns and fantasies about your life become a topic of therapy?

A Voyeuristic Response to an Incest Survivor: A Passage From Christine Courtois

Now in independent practice as a counseling psychologist, Christine Courtois has specialized in understanding the process of sexual victimization and providing help to survivors of sexual assault for more than 3 decades. In 1972, she cofounded (and served as codirector with Ruth Anne Koenick) the University of Maryland's University Women's Crisis Center. Originally a rape crisis center, the facility soon began providing services to women who had experienced—and in some instances, continued to experience—incest. Six years later, Courtois conducted a study of female incest survivors, patterning her research on the studies of battered women conducted by Lenore Walker.

In her book *Healing the Incest Wound: Adult Survivors in Therapy*,[22] Christine Courtois described two types of voyeuristic responses to patients who have endured incest. In the first type, the clinician treats the incest survivor almost as if he or she were a laboratory animal or a visitor from another planet whose primary purpose was to teach the therapist about the exotic, fascinating, and sometimes horrifying topic of forbidden sexual intimacies with a relative. The therapist–client relationship focuses on the client's potential use to the therapist as a teaching vehicle, a means by which the therapist can learn about incest. Courtois observed that some therapists may even thank their clients for being such good educators and sources of information.

> This perspective is dangerous because it encourages the "survivor as heroine" aspect of the incest, minimizes its harmfulness, and recreates the dynamic of the survivor taking care of others, this time the therapist. As one survivor put it: "I parented my parents and thought that was enough. I didn't want to have to teach or take care of my therapist. Her job was to take care of me."
>
> In the second type of privileged voyeurism, the therapist focuses on the sexual aspects and details of the abuse to the exclusion of other issues. Survivors who have experienced this therapist reaction tell of feeling pressured to describe in detail the most intimate and often the most humiliating sexual aspects of the abuse early in treatment to satisfy the therapist's prurient interests. They also describe being made to feel like they are on the witness stand and are constantly redirected from the other issues back to the sexual details. The therapist often appears spellbound or tantalized by the survivor's incest history. Clearly, such behavior is another experience of victimization. (pp. 237–238)

Questions

1. In what ways, if at all, have you used patients as a source of information about forms of victimization, dysfunctional

---

[22]Courtois, C. A. (1988). *Healing the incest wound: Adult survivors in therapy.* New York: W.W. Norton.

processes, or clinical phenomena? How has this process of learning affected the therapy and your relationship with the patient?

2. Have you ever been sexually aroused by a client's description of sexual abuse? How did you respond to the arousal? Do you believe that the client was aware of your arousal?

3. If you have been a patient in therapy, have you ever felt that your therapist was behaving voyeuristically toward you?

4. During clinical supervision, have you ever felt that you were "on the witness stand" and were "constantly redirected from the other issues back to the sexual details" in a way that was at odds with your supervisory needs?

Adjunctive Therapy

You've been working with a client for several years. Over the course of therapy, the client has occasionally, and with great success, undertaken adjunctive therapy. Once the client worked with a specialist in eating disorders. Another time the client worked with a sleep specialist to address chronic insomnia. One day the client says,

> I've decided to do some adjunctive therapy again. I think homosexuality is wrong and I no longer want to be living in sin. I've prayed on this and talked it over with my pastor, who has given me the name of a therapist who specializes in helping people make the change from gay to straight. I have my first session day after tomorrow. I feel so hopeful and relieved.

Questions

1. What feelings did you experience as you read this scenario, imagining yourself to be the therapist?

2. What would you like to say to the client?

3. What do you think you would say to the client?

4. If the client simply made that announcement and then immediately moved on to discuss other issues, would you try to initiate a discussion of this adjunctive therapy? If so, what would you say, and which aspects would you want to discuss?

The Note

You have just completed your third marriage counseling session with a couple that has been together for 4 years. As you walk back to your desk, you find that one of them has left a note for you. Opening the note, you find the client's declaration of overwhelming feelings of love for you, the desire for an affair, and a promise to commit suicide if you tell the other member of the couple about this note.

Questions

1. Would you initially address this matter privately with the client who left the note or with the two clients as a couple? What do you consider as you make this decision?
2. How would your understanding of and response to this client's "love" for you differ, if at all, if you were conducting individual rather than couple counseling?
3. What feelings does the client's threat of suicide evoke in you? How do you address this issue?
4. As you imagine this scenario, do you tend to believe that the other client is aware of his or her partner's loving feelings toward you?
5. When you see a couple in therapy, what ground rules, agreements, or formal contracts do you create regarding confidentiality, "secrets," and the scheduling of sessions with only one member of the couple? Do you provide any of this information in written form?
6. When providing couple counseling, do you keep one chart for the couple or individual charts for the two clients? How do you decide what information should be included in (or excluded from) the charts? Would you include the note described in the scenario in the chart?

Eyes Open

You've been working for a couple of months with a client who has lost both parents within the past year, cannot find work, and is struggling to make ends meet as a single parent. Despite the client's considerable distress, you find it hard to pay attention during the sessions, become bored and sleepy—in fact can hardly keep your eyes open.

Questions

1. What feelings did you experience as you read this scenario?
2. As you imagine yourself as the therapist in this scenario, do you have ideas about why you might be bored and sleepy?
3. What, if anything, would you do in response to your being bored and sleepy?
4. How, if at all, would you chart this?
5. Have you ever felt bored and sleepy with a client? How about in class?
6. How would you respond if the client, while talking about the struggle to make ends meet, suddenly said, "You seem bored and sleepy, as if you can hardly keep your eyes open. Do I bore you? Should I just leave right now?"

No More

You've seen a client for six sessions. The client is impulsive, feels under pressure, becomes drunk once or twice a week, and has been considering suicide (although he or she is not actively suicidal at the moment). You are concerned that there is considerable risk that if therapy is discontinued, the person will commit suicide. Having reviewed your chart notes, both the managed care case reviewer and the reviewer's supervisor (you initiated a formal appeal) disagreed and refused to authorize additional sessions.

Questions

1. What feelings did you experience as you read this scenario, imagining yourself as the therapist?
2. What factors would you consider in deciding how to respond to this situation?
3. What would you like to do in this situation?

4. What do you think you actually would do?
5. If someone else were the therapist in this situation and the client were one of your relatives or loved ones, what would you want the therapist to do?
5. Does this scenario suggest any myths to you?

Your Income

One of your clients works as a prostitute and sells illegal drugs. At the beginning of the third session, the client, while handing over the fee, asks, "Does it bother you at all to take this money earned from prostitution and illegal drugs?"

Questions

1. What feelings did you experience as you read this scenario?
2. What factors would you consider in thinking through how to respond?
3. How do you believe you would respond to the client?
4. Are there any clients whose money you would refuse because of the client's occupation or the source of the money?
5. Does this scenario evoke any of the myths described in chapter 1 or suggest any new ones to you?

Leaving on Vacation

Having been overworked and right on the edge of burnout (or complete breakdown) for weeks, you've barely made it to your annual vacation. You were able to afford your dream vacation only by booking everything months in advance to take advantage of every discount imaginable. It is late Friday afternoon, you've seen your last patient of the day, and a taxi is taking you straight from the office to the airport, running a little late, but you should just catch your flight. As you use your cell phone to check the messages on your answering machine, you hear a client's voice say,

> Thank you so much for trying to help me, but I won't be coming back to therapy. I know we worked out that elaborate plan

for what I was supposed to do if I got overwhelmed and hopeless about my life, but none of that makes any sense now. I know that if we meet again we will just go over the same plan. This all just came to me, and I feel so much more peaceful now. I know you did your best. I don't want you to worry about me or the kids—we'll be fine. Thank you. Goodbye.

Questions

1. What feelings did you experience as you read this scenario?
2. What issues, possibilities, and responsibilities would you consider as you thought through how to respond to this message?
3. How do you believe that you would respond to this message?
4. How would you chart this incident?
5. Have you ever been in a situation that was similar in some ways to this scenario? If so, what were your feelings, what did you do, and what was the result?

Bright, Funny, Articulate, and Likable

You begin working with a new client around issues of performance anxiety. The client is bright, funny, articulate, and likable while talking with you and in other one-on-one and small-group situations but feels nervous when speaking to large groups, a requirement of a new job. You discover that the new job is a highly visible national leadership role with a neo-Nazi organization.

Questions

1. What did you feel as you read this scenario?
2. How would you like to respond in this situation?
3. What factors would you take into account as you considered how to respond?
4. How do you think you would actually respond?
5. Are there any client political affiliations, such as being a neo-Nazi, sets of attitudes or beliefs, or other characteristics that you believe impair your ability to work effectively with a client? If so, what are the characteristics, and how do they impair your ability?

6. Are there any client political affiliations, sets of attitudes or beliefs, or other characteristics that would lead you to refuse to work with a client? If so, what are the characteristics, how would you handle it and chart it if you discovered the characteristic during the initial session, and how would you handle it and chart it if you only discovered it once the therapy were under way?

Normal

A patient tells about a ritual that takes place once a week or so involving a pet dog. The patient strokes the dog in such a way that the dog becomes sexually excited. Then the patient plays with the dog until the patient and then the dog experience an orgasm. The patient asks you if this is normal and if you think it is OK.

Questions

1. What feelings did you experience when you read this scenario?
2. When you first imagined the scenario, what were the patient's gender, age, cultural background, race, sexual orientation, and socioeconomic status? Is the patient you imagined attractive to you? How is the patient dressed? What other attributions would you make about this patient based only on the information provided in the scenario?
3. If the patient had a different gender, age, race, sexual orientation, socioeconomic status, and cultural background than you first imagined, would your feelings change? How?
4. Are you likely to reveal your feelings about the ritual to the patient? Would you give a prompt and direct answer to the patient's question? If so, what would you consider saying? If not, why not? Would you state your intention not to answer, or would you simply not answer (e.g., remain silent, provide information that is not responsive to the question, respond to the patient's question with a question of your own)?

5. Over the course of your life, have your beliefs about what is sexually "normal" and "OK" or your understanding of those two concepts remained relatively stable or changed considerably? How do your own beliefs about what is "normal" and "OK" affect the work you do and your relationships with patients?

Fantasizing Love and Marriage With a Patient: A Passage From Harold Searles

Describing his own experiences with love in the countertransference, Harold Searles[23] contrasted his reactions to two of his patients at the Chestnut Lodge Research Institute in Rockville, Maryland. During his first few years at Chestnut Lodge, Searles treated a man in his mid-30s who was diagnosed with paranoid schizophrenia. During the second year of treatment, he became aware that he was experiencing romantic and sexual feelings about his patient. These feelings made him quite anxious. He almost panicked when, during one of the sessions, he and the patient were sitting silently, listening to a sweetly romantic song playing on a distant radio, "when I suddenly felt that this man was dearer to me than anyone else in the world, including my wife" (p. 185). His reaction to his patient (or to his feelings about his patient) made him so uncomfortable that, upon a variety of pretexts, he was soon no longer working with the man.

Years later, once he had worked through his discomfort through his own analysis, Searles began working with another patient whom he described as extremely unattractive in dress and physical appearance, at least according to conventional standards, and as having a severe disorder. The first 2 years of therapy were marked by substantial negative transference and countertransference. Gradually, however, Searles found himself attracted to the patient. "One morning, as I was putting on a carefully-selected necktie, I realized that I was putting it on for him" (p. 185).[24]

---

[23]Searles, H. F. (1959). Oedipal love in the countertransference. *International Journal of Psychoanalysis, 40,* 180–190.

[24]See footnote 23, this chapter.

During the next 2 years of treatment, the patient described the relationship as "being married" and told of his fantasies of marrying his therapist. One day, as Searles and the patient were riding in a car, Searles enjoyed a fantasy that he and the patient were engaged to be married. He imagined what the future might be like if he and the patient were to go on shopping trips together and to share experiences common to loving couples.

> When I drove home from work at the end of the day I was filled with a poignant realization of how utterly and tragically unrealizable were the desires of this man who had been hospitalized continually, now, for fourteen years. But I felt that, despite the tragic aspect of this, what we were going through was an essential, constructive part of what his recovery required; these needs of his would have to be experienced, I felt, in however unrecognizable a form at first, so that they could become reformulated, in the course of our work, into channels which would lead to greater possibilities for gratification. (p. 185)[25]

Questions

1. Does your ability to recognize, acknowledge, accept, and understand your attraction to a client depend at all on the gender of the client?
2. Does your ability to discuss your feelings of attraction in supervision or case conferences depend at all on the gender of the client?
3. Have you ever fantasized marriage with a same-sex client? With an opposite-sex client? What feelings did these fantasies evoke in you? Do you believe that the client in such fantasies was aware of your feelings about him or her?
4. Have you ever been aware of wanting to refer or terminate a client because your reactions to the client made you anxious? What did you do?
5. Have you ever been repulsed by a client's physical appearance? How did your reaction affect the therapy and your

---

[25]See footnote 23, this chapter.

relationship with the client? Do you think that the client
was aware of your reaction?

6. Have you ever been surprised as your feelings about a client changed over the course of therapy? Have you ever
found it difficult to acknowledge these changes?

Saved!

Your practice was thriving, and you were doing quite well finan-
cially until you got the bright idea of starting a restaurant. The
restaurant bombed, and the lease payments on the property have
eaten all your savings and are threatening to send you into bankruptcy. You advertise the property, but month after month goes
by without anyone expressing any interest. Just as you're about
to declare bankruptcy, your realtor calls to tell you that a buyer
has emerged who is not interested in bargaining about the price
but is eager to pay the full asking price to obtain the property.
Later that day, you discover that the buyer is one of your therapy
patients, the one who is always trying to give you expensive gifts
and for whom the focus of therapy has been a compulsion to try
to please you.

Questions

1. What feelings did you experience as you read this scenario?
2. What would you like to do in this situation?
3. What issues would you consider as you think through how
   to respond?
4. What do you think you would actually do?
5. How would you chart this matter?

The Security Guard

You work as a therapist for a mental health clinic. At the end of
the day, you are asked to stop by the administrator's office before
you leave. The administrator tells you that the clinic is being re-
structured to de-emphasize individual therapy. Clients who have

been in individual therapy will be evaluated to see whether they need further therapy and, if so, will be admitted to therapy groups. As a result of the restructuring, they will not be needing as many therapists, and you are one of the excellent clinicians they will, with great regret and best wishes for future success, be letting go. You'll be receiving 6 weeks of severance pay, once you sign some paperwork, and today was your last day. They will, of course, be providing you with solid recommendations should they receive inquiries from potential employers. A security guard will escort you now to clean out your desk and leave the premises. You are not to return. The locks will be changed at the end of the day, once everyone leaves. The security guard will provide you with the phone number of an "outplacement consultant" whom you may wish to contact, should you find that helpful.

Questions

1. What feelings did you experience as you read this scenario?
2. What was your first impulse when you finished reading the scenario?
3. What issues would you consider as you thought through how to respond?
4. How do you believe that you would respond?
5. If you were one of the clients, what would you want the therapist to do?
6. As you read this scenario, did any myths described in chapter 1 or any other myths come to mind?

The Partner

You have been working with a battered woman whose partner has terrorized her for years, micromanaging her life and threatening to kill her if she ever crosses him. The partner, a former soldier who taught both hand-to-hand and firearm combat techniques in the military, maintains an extensive collection of guns and continues to engage in paramilitary training and exercises. The battered woman has managed to keep secret from the partner that she is in therapy—something likely to drive the partner over the edge, she said—by arranging with a sympathetic employer to slip out for an hour session once a week. She begins a session by saying, "I think that this morning my partner may have found out I'm in therapy with you and where your office is. I don't know, but I think I may have been followed here."

Questions

1. What feelings did you experience as you read this scenario?
2. What was your first impulse as you finished reading the scenario?
3. What factors would you consider as you decided how to respond to this situation?
4. How do you think you would respond?
5. Does this scenario seem related to any myths discussed in chapter 1 or any other myths?

A Therapist Unaware of the Client's Attraction: A Passage From Marny Hall

Marny Hall[26] described vividly the ways in which clients may fear and be uncomfortable with sexual attraction to their therapists. She described, for example, one man who took elaborate steps to ensure that he would not be attracted to his therapist. He went out of his way to select a therapist who did not have the physical characteristics that he found attractive. By the second therapy session, however, he was experiencing an elaborate sexual fantasy about the therapist. In the following passage, Hall described a different situation in which the therapist remains unaware that her female client is intensely attracted to her.

> Sky was so attracted to Cecile, her therapist, that she drove by her house frequently, hoping to catch a glimpse. She called Cecile late at night and hung up when she answered. After three months of this (all of which remained unknown to Cecile), Sky decided that her feelings were hopeless and she stopped therapy. (p. 152)

---

[26]Hall, M. (1985). *The lavender couch: A consumer's guide to psychotherapy for lesbians and gay men*. Boston: Alyson.

Questions

1. To what degree do you think that a therapist's physical attributes are important in eliciting a patient's sexual attraction?
2. Have you ever felt that you were unusually slow in discovering that a patient was sexually attracted to you? In thinking about it later, were there subtle—or not so subtle—signs of the patient's attraction that you failed to notice or make sense of? Were there any personal factors that made it difficult for you to recognize these signs?
3. What behaviors have patients used to express their attraction to you? Have any of these ever frightened you?
4. As a therapist, have you ever had a patient stop therapy without explanation? Why do you think he or she withdrew? What did you do? What other approaches might you have used?
5. Have you ever experienced "hang up" phone calls that you thought might be made by a particular patient? How did you feel? How did you decide whether to raise the issue with the patient?

Diagnosis

You meet for the first time with a new client who has just retired after 30 years of working for the same company. The client, who is agitated, desperate, and despairing, has just learned that because of bad investments and sloppy accounting, the pension plan is worthless and the money counted on for retirement is gone. It is clear to you that the client's condition is not covered by the client's health insurance; however, if you fill in a false diagnosis, the client will qualify for once-a-week therapy sessions.

Questions

1. What feelings did you experience as you read this scenario?
2. What was your initial impulse when you finished reading the scenario?
3. What issues would you consider as you decided what to do?
4. Under what circumstances, if any, would you submit a false diagnosis?

5. Under what circumstances, if any, would you consider filing a false diagnosis to be insurance fraud?
6. Under what circumstances, if any, do you believe a therapist should record false information about a client in the client's chart, insurance forms, or other documentation?
7. Under what circumstances, if any, do you believe that a clinical or administrative supervisor should record false information about a supervisee?
8. Does this scenario seem related to any myths?

Size

During your first session with a new patient, he tells you that he has always been concerned that his penis was too small. Suddenly, he pulls down his pants and asks you if you think it is too small. (Consider the same scenario with a new patient who is concerned about the size of her breasts.)

Questions

1. What would you, as therapist, want to do first? Why? What do you think you would do first? Why?
2. What difference would it make if this were a patient whom you had been treating for a year rather than a new patient?
3. How, if at all, would your feelings and actions be different according to whether treatment was conducted on an inpatient or an outpatient basis?
4. How, if at all, would your feelings and actions differ according to the gender of the patient?
5. Imagine that the male and female patients in the scenario are 15 years old. What feelings does the scenario evoke in you? What do you do? What fantasies occur to you about what might happen after the event described in the scenario?

Recordings and Photographs

In the midst of a therapy that has lasted about 8 months, the client remarks, "I find it helpful to listen to our sessions later." When you look puzzled, the client explains,

Oh, didn't I tell you? I've been recording all our sessions. I have a complete library of them at home. When my friends ask what I do at therapy, I'm able to keep them up-to-date. Sometimes I take pictures of you on my cell phone here.

Questions

1. How did you feel as you read this scenario?
2. What was your first impulse after you finished reading it?
3. What issues would you consider in thinking through how to respond?
4. How do you believe you would respond to this client?
5. How would you chart this material?
6. What myths, if any, seem related to this scenario?

A Different Direction

You are in the midst of your internship and working with a suicidal client. Your supervisor, the internship director who will be vouching for your hours when you apply for licensure and writing a key letter of recommendation when you apply for jobs, outlines an approach for you to take. You are convinced, however, that the supervisor is wrong and that the approach will make the client quit therapy and perhaps commit suicide. You respectfully but persistently describe your reservations and the approach you believe that this client needs, but your supervisor is adamant and insists that you follow her or his approach.

Questions

1. What feelings did you experience when you read this scenario?
2. What was your initial impulse after reading it?
3. What possible options would you consider?
4. What issues and possible consequences would you consider?
5. What do you think you would do in this situation?
6. Under what circumstances, if any, do you believe that a therapist should refuse to do what a supervisor directs the

therapist to do? If there are such cases, under what circumstances, if any, should the therapist not inform the
supervisor about taking a different course of action than
the supervisor directed?

7. Under what circumstances, if any, do you believe it is legitimate for a therapist to withhold information from a
supervisor?

8. Under what circumstances, if any, do you believe it is legitimate for a supervisor to withhold information from a
therapist?

Research Data

Your client, a prominent psychologist, describes having faked data
on several research studies, whose results were hailed as
groundbreaking and became widely accepted and influential (e.g.,
in textbooks, forensic cases). The client has no regrets, believes
that these studies helped move the field in a positive direction,
sees no reason to discontinue the practice, and does not wish to
discuss the matter further.

Questions

1. What feelings did you experience as you read this scenario?
2. What was your first impulse when you finished reading
the scenario?
3. What issues and possible consequences would you consider as you thought through how to respond?
4. How do you think you would respond?
5. Does this scenario seem related to any myths that were
discussed in chapter 1 or to any other myths?

The Right Stuff

You've just taken over as director of one of the units at a high-
end therapy clinic, known for its celebrity clientele. It's a job you
treasure because it enables you to support your family, and in a
tight job market it would be hard for you to find other work as a

clinician. In addition to providing therapy and supervision on the unit, you'll be responsible for hiring and firing staff. The clinic's CEO has a long private talk with you about how the staff must project a certain image and must be the kind of people with whom the clinic's select clientele will be comfortable. From that point on in the conversation, nothing is said directly but it is made absolutely clear to you that to keep your job, you must never hire anyone who is even 10 pounds overweight, must never hire anyone from certain racial and ethnic groups, must never hire anyone with a physical or mental disability, and must keep scrupulous records so that no formal complaint of discrimination could ever be sustained and must emphasize to the public that the clinic is an equal opportunity employer.

Questions

1. What did you feel as you read this scenario?
2. What thoughts would be running through your mind in this situation?
3. Does this scenario suggest any myths?
4. What would you like to do if you were in this situation?
5. What do you think you would do if you were in this situation?

The Party

A couple you know gives wonderful dinner parties. Every party is different but a typical night might start with drinks around 5 o'clock, followed by some silly game like charades for half an hour or so, a many-course meal of excellent food and wine, and then retiring to the living room to talk long into the night. You accept an invitation, and when you show up, you discover there are the two hosts and four guests, including a couple that has lived together for several years, you, and your therapy client who has been working through an intense erotic transference to you.

Questions

1. How did you feel after reading this scenario?

2. What was your first impulse when you finished reading the scenario?
3. What possible courses of action would you consider?
4. What issues and possible consequences would you consider?
5. What do you think you would do?

Misusing the Borderline Diagnosis: A Passage From David Reiser and Hanna Levenson

In a provocative article, "Abuses of the Borderline Diagnosis: A Clinical Problem With Teaching Opportunities," David Reiser and Hanna Levenson[27] explored six ways in which the diagnosis of borderline personality disorder is often misapplied. These abuses include using a borderline diagnosis to avoid working with a client's sexual issues, to cover the therapist's sloppy diagnostic procedures, to rationalize a lack of success in the treatment, to prevent the use of psychopharmacological or other medical interventions that might be of help to the patient, to express the therapist's countertransference hatred, and to rationalize the therapist's acting out.

In the following case history, Reiser and Levenson suggested that the therapist's sexual attraction to the patient led to his acting out and to his misuse of the borderline diagnosis. His difficulty accepting his attraction caused him to "freeze up." The authors described how the "therapist held back from an unusually attractive patient and refused to be human when she requested empathy and advice" (p. 1530).[28] A brief summary of the treatment sessions follows.

A psychiatry resident began work with a college senior, described by clinicians on the unit as "strikingly beautiful" (p. 1530).[29] She had sought therapy because she had suffered a variety of traumatic events. An automobile crash had killed one of her close friends. Marijuana possession had led to the arrest of

---

[27]Reiser, D. E., & Levenson, H. (1984). Abuses of the borderline diagnosis: A clinical problem with teaching opportunities. *American Journal of Psychiatry, 141,* 1528–1532.

[28]See footnote 27, this chapter.

[29]See footnote 27, this chapter.

her brother, who had entered mandated drug treatment. Her parents' marriage was troubled, and divorce seemed imminent.

The young woman cried as she described these situations. She told the therapist that she felt guilty, that her mother looked to her for answers. She asked the therapist to help her decide what she should say to her mother.

Throughout the woman's account, the therapist maintained a blank silence. When asked a question, he did not reply but remained silent. Finally, he spoke. He asked the woman to describe her current feelings about her brother and then to describe her feelings about her brother at the time of his birth.

The patient attempted to comply with the resident's request but repeatedly returned to her question: How could she respond to her mother who seemed to put the entire burden for solving the family's problems on the patient's shoulders? The therapist neither addressed the woman's question nor acknowledged that she was clearly distressed by the traumatic events and by her feelings that she must "make things right" for her mother.

The patient arrived on time for her second appointment, but the therapist did not appear. He had marked down the wrong date in his appointment book. The patient came back for one more session, during which the resident was again distant and aloof. Subsequently the patient cancelled all further appointments. The resident stated, "I think she was probably borderline" (p. 1530).[30]

Questions

1. Have you ever experienced an incident with a client in which you felt "frozen"? What caused you to "freeze up"?
2. What aspects of a client's attractiveness or sexuality do you find most threatening, anxiety provoking, or difficult to acknowledge?
3. What aspects of your own sexuality do you find most threatening, anxiety provoking, or difficult to acknowledge?
4. Has someone's attractiveness or sexuality ever evoked an angry response from you? Has it ever caused you to be inhibited and to lack spontaneity?

---

[30]See footnote 27, this chapter.

5. What aspect of your response to an attractive client would you find most difficult to discuss with your clinical supervisor or a colleague consultant?
6. Have you ever declined to treat a patient because he or she was too sexually attractive to you?

A Strong Reaction

A client brags about stealing from his business partners. He mocks their trust. He describes in detail the wonderful gifts he gives to his "girlfriends" and how he gives a cheaper version of the gifts to his wife. He never goes to events involving his children, such as school plays or sports, because they are "a waste of time." He recounts several occasions when he has lied to his friends to get something that he wanted from them. You realize after seeing this client for several weeks that you hate him.

Questions

1. What feelings did you experience as you read this scenario?
2. What issues and possible consequences would you consider as you thought through how to respond to your hating this client?
3. What possible courses of action would you consider?
4. What do you think you would do?
5. How would you chart this matter?
6. Do you believe that hating a client impairs your ability to work competently with that person? If so, how?
7. Have you ever hated a client? If so, why, what did you do, and what happened?

Medication

You and a client with whom you have been working for 4 months both agree that medication might be helpful, so you refer the client to a psychiatrist you trust, an expert in psychotropic medications, for a consult. The client later sends you a brief note terminating therapy with you because he or she is beginning therapy with the psychiatrist.

Questions

1. What feelings did you experience when you read this scenario?
2. What was your first impulse after reading it?
3. What courses of action would be open to you in this situation?
4. What issues and possible consequences would you consider when thinking through this situation?
5. What do you think you would do?
6. If another therapist referred a client with whom they were working to you for a brief consult and the client told you that he or she had decided to transfer to you, under what circumstances, if any, would you agree to begin therapy with the client?

A Client Becomes Aroused When Her Therapist Comes to Her Home: A Passage From Helen Block Lewis

Helen Block Lewis[31] described a pivotal event in her treatment of a young woman she called Z. Z had sought treatment for a drinking problem that was causing her to miss work. She shared an apartment with her lover, but from time to time would become drunk and pick up a male or female stranger for a "one-night stand."

During the course of therapy, Z separated from her lover and moved into her own apartment. According to Lewis, her shame and guilt caused her to feel angry at her therapist for encouraging her to live by herself. During a session, she expressed this anger, which Lewis attempted to recognize and interpret. Nevertheless, Lewis noticed that she herself seemed impatient and even somewhat scornful during this session, from which the patient left offended. Lewis further revealed that her own impatience led her to feel guilty. Then, in response to her own guilt as a therapist for the way she'd handled the session, she felt anxious.

---

[31]Lewis, H. B. (1971). *Shame and guilt in neurosis.* New York: International Universities Press.

This hour was the last session of the week, to be followed by a three-day weekend. On Saturday evening I had a desperate call from Z, who was drunk and weeping hysterically. I arrived at her apartment and found her half naked and disheveled, trying to sober up. She had begun to drink on awakening in the morning and had "perversely" and "defiantly" (her phrasing) continued all day. Pathetically, she wanted to "free-associate," now that I had come, in order to find out immediately why all this had happened. When I said I thought she needed at the moment to rest and recover herself, she was, typically, rebuffed. She then told me that she was sexually excited and wanted to make love to me. I reminded her that sexual excitement often followed her humiliation at feeling neglected. Again she was rebuffed, but appeared calmer. It was apparent that my presence was somewhat irksome to her, that it embarrassed her. I suggested that she tell me when she was ready for me to leave. She demurred, but shook hands a few minutes later and saw me to the door. (p. 452)[32]

Questions

1. Reread the passage, but substitute a male for a female therapist. Does this make any difference in your understanding of the events or the feelings the passage evokes in you?
2. Reread the passage, but substitute a male for a female patient. Does this make any difference in your understanding of the events or the feelings the passage evokes in you?
3. Imagine that you are the therapist in this passage. What thoughts occur to you about the patient being half naked? Do you mention or address this in any way? Do you feel any impulse or make any effort to ask her to put on more clothes?
4. If you were the therapist is this passage, could you imagine any possibility that you might feel angry with this patient? If so, why? How would you respond to your feelings of anger?
5. If you were the therapist in this passage, could you image any possibility that you might become sexually aroused? If so, why? How would you respond to your feelings of arousal?

---

[32]See footnote 31, this chapter.

6. If you were the therapist in this passage, what would you consider in deciding what to include and what to exclude as you made your notes in the patient's chart?
7. If you were the therapist in this passage, what thoughts would you have about the next session with Z?
8. If you were the therapist in this passage, what thoughts would you have about how to respond to Z's phone call? Would it make any difference if Z had called and told you that she had taken an overdose of a drug?
9. Does this passage evoke any of the myths described in chapter 1 or suggest any new myths to you?

Descriptions

A client begins describing sexual fantasies in great detail. You find that you become sexually aroused and are blushing. The patient notices that you seem different somehow and asks you, "What's wrong?"

Questions

1. Is it likely that you will respond to the client's question directly? Why or why not?
2. What would you consider as you decide what to do next?
3. As you imagine yourself becoming sexually aroused in front of a patient, what feelings do you experience? Would you mention these feelings to the client? To a supervisor? To a colleague? To a supervisee?
4. As you imagine yourself blushing in front of a client, what feelings do you experience? Would you reveal these feelings to the client? To a supervisor? To a colleague? To a supervisee?
5. What effects do you imagine your arousal and blushing might have had on the client?
6. As you first imagined this scenario, was the client sexually aroused while describing the fantasies?
7. Are you aware of any desire for the client to continue describing the fantasies? Any desire to move closer to the client? Any desire to extend the length of the session? Any desire that the session were already over? Any desire that

the client had not described the fantasies in such detail? Any wish that you had met this client outside the therapeutic relationship so that you could enjoy a sexually intimate relationship? Any desire to terminate or transfer this client?

8. The session is now over, and you are preparing to meet with your supervisor. Are you any more eager or reluctant to meet with your supervisor than you customarily would be? Do you believe that you would describe the client's fantasies in great detail to your supervisor? Would you mention your own sexual arousal to your supervisor?

9. You describe this session to a colleague. The colleague says, "I think you must have been acting seductively. In some subtle ways, you must have been giving signals encouraging the client to talk in a way that would stimulate you sexually." What do you feel when your colleague says this? What do you think?

10. You describe this session to a colleague. The colleague says, "I think this client was trying to seduce you." What do you feel when your colleague says this? What do you think?

11. You describe this session to a colleague. The colleague says, "Aren't you concerned that this client might file a complaint against you for sexual misconduct?" What do you feel when your colleague says this? What do you think?

12. You describe this session to a colleague. The colleague says, "Some people have all the luck. I wish one of my clients would do that!" What do you feel when your colleague says this? What do you think?

13. When a client describes sexual fantasies in great detail, under what circumstances might you fail to include any mention of the topic in the client's chart? Under what circumstances might you include detailed descriptions of the fantasies in the chart? What are your feelings and thoughts as you anticipate the possible consequences of including or omitting sexual material while charting?

14. You are now sitting in your office 5 minutes before the next session with this client. Do you find yourself either more or less eager to meet with this client than you usually are?

15. In future sessions, would you make any effort to encourage or discourage the client from describing sexual fantasies in great detail?

A Suicidal Client

A client with few financial resources is in a constant struggle with suicidal thoughts and impulses. Ambivalent about therapy, the client continues to stay with it on a day-to-day basis, in part to sustain a fragile link with you, whom the client views as "my only lifeline." The client has a terrible body odor that lingers in your office for hours after the client's session. Air freshener has little effect.

Questions

1. What feelings did you experience as you read this scenario, imagining yourself as the therapist?
2. What was your first impulse after reading it?
3. What possible courses of action would you consider?
4. What issues and possible consequences would you focus on when considering how to respond?
5. How do you think you would respond?
6. How, if at all, would your response be different if it were your supervisor rather than your client who had the odor?

The Newspaper

You've been working with a client who has been anxious and depressed for 3 months and the therapy, weekly sessions on an outpatient basis, seems to be going well. In fact, you presented the case at a local hospital's grand rounds as an example of how you believe therapists can best form a working relationship with clients who are suicidal. You look at the morning newspaper and discover that your client has committed suicide by jumping from the top of your office building.

Questions

1. What feelings did you experience as you read this scenario, imagining yourself as the therapist?
2. What thoughts do you experience as you imagine yourself to be the therapist in this scenario?

3. How do you imagine your colleagues would respond to you if a client you were working with committed suicide? Do you believe that any of them would be critical of you, either to your face or behind your back?

4. To what extent do you believe that therapists should be held accountable for adequately assessing their clients' risk of suicide and for adequately intervening (e.g., hospitalizing the client) if the client is at risk for suicide? Do you believe that the standard of care, as it is legally enforced, is realistic?

5. If a client you were working with committed suicide, to what degree, if at all, would that be a traumatic event for you? What steps, if any, would you take under such circumstances to take care of yourself and to ensure that you could continue to work (or return to work) competently?

Instructing a Client to Imagine Her Breasts Tingling: A Passage From Theodore Barber

Ted Barber[33] conducted extensive research and wrote prolifically on the phenomenon of hypnosis. In a review chapter, he described studies conducted by several other specialists in hypnosis to help women develop larger breasts through hypnosis. The women were given a version of the following instructions:

> Imagine that the sun (or a heat lamp) is shining on the breasts or that wet, warm towels are on the breasts and feel the heat as it flows through the breasts; imagine the breasts growing, as they did during puberty, and experience the feelings of tenderness, swelling, and tightness of the skin over the breasts; and imagine that the breasts are becoming warm, tingling, pulsating, sensitive, and that they are growing. (p. 85)

In considering the nature of such techniques, Barber suggested that it would be useful to examine the extent to which the tech-

---

[33]Barber, T. X. (1984). Changing "unchangeable" bodily processes by (hypnotic) suggestions: A new look at hypnosis, cognitions, imaging, and the mind–body problem. In A. A. Sheikh (Ed.), *Imagination and healing* (pp. 69–127). Farmingdale, NY: Baywood.

niques involved sexual arousal. "When women are given suggestions by men to relax, let go, and imagine the breasts tingling, pulsating, and growing, they might recall or imagine sexual situations which could produce sexual arousal" (p. 86).[34]

Questions

1. As you imagine yourself giving hypnotic suggestions for a woman's breasts to feel warm, tingly, and so on, do you feel sexually aroused? Do you think that the patient might be aware of your feelings? If so, how might she feel?
2. Do you feel more comfortable giving suggestions that might cause sexual arousal to men or to women? Why?
3. Do you ever feel concerned that when giving hypnotic (or other therapeutic) suggestions that might have an erotic element, you might become tongue-tied or embarrassed? Has this ever happened to you?
4. To what extent do you consider your patients' values, morals, or mores when you speak of their breasts or genitals?
5. How do you choose which words to use when speaking of a patient's genitals or erotic behaviors? Do you ever use words that are different from those that the patient tends to use?
6. Do the words you use in the presence of the patient about the patient's genitals or erotic behaviors tend to be the same or to differ from the words you use for these sexual organs and activities when discussing the treatment with your supervisor?
7. What myths about psychologists, if any, does this passage bring to mind?

Feeling Safe

For about 6 months, you've been working with a client who spends much of each day in a boiling rage that sometimes seems almost out of control. One day the client says, "You know what makes me feel safe?" She then reaches down into a briefcase and pulls

---

[34]See footnote 33, this chapter.

out a gun. "I always have it handy and always keep it loaded. I've rarely had to use it, but when I did, I never regretted it and the person never bothered me or anyone else again."

Questions

1. What were your feelings as you read this scenario?
2. What were your thoughts as you read this scenario?
3. What was your first impulse after reading this scenario?
4. What issues and possible consequences would you consider as you thought through how to respond in this situation?
5. How do you believe you would respond?
6. Has any client ever frightened you? If so, what happened?
7. To what degree, if any, does fear interfere with your ability to work competently?
8. If you become too frightened to work competently, what steps do you take?
9. What steps do you take to ensure you are safe as you work?

Pleasing a Husband

Your patient describes her troubled marriage to you. Her husband used to get mad and hit her—"not too hard," she says—but he's pretty much gotten over that. Their sex life is not good. Her husband enjoys anal intercourse, but she finds it frightening and painful. She tells you that she'd like to explore her resistance to this form of sexual behavior in her therapy. Her goal is to become comfortable engaging in the behavior so that she can please her husband, enjoy sex with him, and have a happy marriage.

Questions

1. As you imagine yourself as the therapist in this scenario, what are you feeling when the patient says that her husband used to get mad and hit her? What are you thinking?
2. What are you feeling when she says that she finds anal intercourse frightening and painful? What are you thinking?

3. What do you feel when she describes her goals in therapy? What are you thinking?
4. In what ways do you believe that your feelings may influence how you proceed with this patient?
5. Does this scenario evoke with any myths about psychotherapists that were discussed in chapter 1 or any other myths?

7

Confronting an Impasse: What Do We Do When We Don't Know What to Do?

What *do* we do when we don't know what to do?

The taboo topics of our profession—those issues we learn to stay away from, to pretend aren't there or aren't relevant, to avoid exploring or engaging—and the myths that help sustain them can impair our ability to handle uncertainty.

A temporary "not knowing what to do" can freeze into a seemingly permanent paralyzing impasse. It can touch off all sorts of alarm bells and red flags—that we are not competent, that we are not intelligent, that we are not meant to do this work, that we are not well trained, that others will think we're incompetent, that we're sure to be sued, that we'll be thrown out of school, fired, or our referrals will dry up. So we may tend to ignore, deny, discount, distract—or just jump toward any alternative to relieve ourselves of the burdens of not knowing. We tend not to explore the taboo topics, the myths, or whatever it is that plays a role in our not knowing what to do. We may avoid the steps that might be helpful in finding a valid, constructive, useful way out of the impasse.

A repeated theme of this book is that there are no one-size-fits-all ways to approach taboo topics and other uncomfortable issues, to understand their nature and implications for therapy. Various theoretical orientations provide different, sometimes opposing ways of approaching such questions. Each person and situation is unique. Each therapist must explore and achieve a working understanding of the unfolding situation and his or her role in and reaction to it. A "cookbook" approach can undermine this process.

The main assumption of this book is that the individual therapist, adequately trained and consulting with colleagues, can be trusted to draw his or her own conclusions. But there are times when we—well, most of us—reach an impasse and just don't know what to do. For example, our best understanding of the situation may suggest a course of action that seems productive yet questionable and potentially harmful. To refrain from a contemplated action may shut the door to our spontaneity, creativity, intuition, and ability to help; to refrain may stunt the patient's progress or impede recovery. To engage in the contemplated action, however, may lead to disaster. It may be helpful for therapists, having reached an impasse, to consider the following steps.

There is nothing extraordinary about these steps. They tend to be routine in ordinary circumstances. But when we feel trapped in an impasse, they are easy to forget.

Consulting

Is there a compelling reason for *not* discussing the contemplated action with a colleague, consultant, or supervisor? One red flag to the possibility that a course of action is inappropriate, that we've stumbled across a taboo, or that we've encountered an issue that triggers exceptional discomfort in us is our reluctance to disclose it to others. One question a therapist may ask about any proposed action is this: If I took this action, would I have any reluctance for all of my professional colleagues to know that I had taken it? If the answer is yes, the reasons are worth examining. If the answer is no, it is worth considering whether one has adequately taken advantage of the opportunities to discuss the matter with a trusted colleague. If discussion with a colleague has not helped to clarify the issues, consultation with other professionals, each of whom may provide different perspectives and suggestions, may be useful.

Reflecting on why and how we are seeking consultation can be an important part of the consultation process. In times of temptation, we may lean toward superficial, phony, or pro forma consultation as a way to get approval or "permission" for a questionable behavior. The apparent consultation is an attempt to silence doubts rather than to explore them. Methods for selecting potential consultants can affect the integrity of the consultation process. Only the least persistent therapist would be unable to find, in a moderate or large community, a consultant who would say "yes" to virtually any proposed intervention. Survey research, for example, suggests that there is a tiny, atypical minority of therapists who even believe that sexual involvement with clients is therapeutic.[1]

Making use of consultation as a regular component of clinical activities rather than as a resource used only on atypical occasions is one way to extend the learning process beyond the time span of the specific study group in which this book served as a focus of exploration and discovery. Regular consultation with a variety of colleagues can strengthen the sense of community in which therapists work. It can provide a safety net, helping us to make sure that our work does not fall into needless errors, unintentional malpractice, or harmful actions due to lack of knowledge, guidance, perspective, challenge, or support. It can create the sense of a cooperative venture in which the process of professional development, exploration, and discovery continue.

Competence

Has the situation moved, perhaps gradually and subtly, into areas beyond our competence? The client may have been referred to us because of an area in which we specialize. The initial sessions focused on this specialized area. But then other problems and factors became apparent, issues in which we've had virtually no education, training, or supervised experience. Suddenly, we're adrift.

Recognizing when we're moving beyond our areas of basic competence can help us find our way out of a seemingly permanent

---

[1]Pope, K. S. (1994). *Sexual involvement with therapists: Patient assessment, subsequent therapy, forensics.* Washington, DC: American Psychological Association.

impasse and avoid impulsive interventions that are tempting but disastrous.

As an extreme example, consider a hypothetical male therapist who discovers, in the second month of work with a patient, that the patient is the victim of childhood sexual abuse. The patient says that he or she fears the therapist and finds it difficult to talk because sexual memories keep intruding. The therapist has listened to colleagues discuss "reenactment therapy" and decides that this might be an appropriate intervention to try on a trial basis with this patient. He asks the patient to describe the memory, which involved anal intercourse. The therapist then suggests that he and the patient get down on the floor, fully clothed, to pantomime the action. Although the therapist has no real knowledge of "reenactment therapy," the approach seems to make sense to him in light of his knowledge of learning theory and behavior therapy. He believes that reenacting the traumatic memory through pantomime, in the safety and security of the therapy office, will enable the patient to become systematically desensitized to the traumatic associations. He anticipates that after one or two slow, careful, reenactments, the patient will no longer generalize the learned fear (as well as other negative feelings) to the therapist. Especially if they are knowledgeable about interventions for people who were sexually abused as children, readers will probably be able to envision some possibly disastrous consequences of the therapist's contemplated actions in this scenario.

Charting

Reviewing the client's chart can suggest a way out of the impasse, or at least the factors that brought us to the impasse. Does the chart seem to reflect accurately and realistically what you know about the client and the nature of your work with the client so far? Are there obvious omissions or significant aspects that have been minimized, swept aside, or distorted? Were any aspects of the referral questions (if any), the client's initial statement of the problem (i.e., reason for seeking professional help), assessment issues, or treatment plan not followed up? Were there any themes that seemed to stop abruptly, any matters that you had intended to explore later that have still not been clarified or addressed? Does any of the information in the chart now seem, in retrospect, to be questionable or to take on different meanings and implications?

When unsure about whether to try an intervention, considering how it will be charted can help us to decide whether to proceed. Is there any hesitance to chart, completely and accurately, what you plan to do, why, and the full array of possible consequences? As suggested in the 1986 book, *Sexual Intimacies Between Therapists and Patients*,[2] thinking a possible intervention through from a future perspective on a "worst possible case" basis can play a useful role in our considerations. That is to say, imaginatively project yourself into the future, imagine that you have tried the intervention with the client and not only did it not have the desired effects but it produced the worst array of consequences that you can imagine this specific intervention could realistically cause. In light of these possible negative consequences, do you believe that the intervention is not only worth trying but also the best available option at this time?

Uncharacteristic Behaviors

Noticing uncharacteristic behaviors can lead to the discovery of how an impasse developed and, sometimes, a constructive way out. Have we been acting in any way, or considering using an intervention, that is substantially outside the range of our usual behaviors? There is, of course, no suggestion that an unusual behavior is per se wrong than there is that it is per se appropriate. Unusual behaviors are, paradoxically, not unusual. The creative therapist will likely try creative interventions. The typical therapist, if there is such a person, will likely engage in atypical behaviors from time to time. But possible actions that seem considerably outside the therapist's general approaches probably warrant special consideration.

For most therapists, therapy is conducted in the consulting room. Some theoretical orientations, however, may not preclude

---

[2]Pope, K. S., & Bouhoutsos, J. C. (1986). *Sexual intimacies between therapists and patients*. New York: Praeger/Greenwood.

the therapist who typically works in the consulting room or hospital from seeing a patient outside those settings if there is clear clinical need and justification. For example, Michael Stone[3] described a woman diagnosed with schizophrenia who was hospitalized during a psychotic break. The woman heaped verbal abuse on her therapist, claiming that the therapist did not really care about her. Then the patient disappeared from the unit.

> The therapist, upon hearing the news, got into her car and canvassed all the bars and social clubs in Greenwich Village which her patient was known to frequent. At about midnight, she found her patient and drove her back to the hospital. From that day forward, the patient grew calmer, less impulsive, and made great progress in treatment. Later, after making substantial recovery, she told her therapist that all the interpretations during the first few weeks in the hospital meant very little to her. But after the "midnight rescue mission" it was clear, even to her, how concerned and sincere her therapist had been from the beginning. (p. 171)

Searching for a patient outside the hospital or office is an extremely atypical event for most therapists. When the therapist undertakes such an atypical action, is it clear that such out-of-the-office contact is warranted by the patient's clinical needs and situation? Actions that are out of the ordinary invite extremely careful evaluation.

It may be helpful to go beyond examination of an unusual behavior to a more complex exploration—the factors that define, reflect, or influence our "usual" behavior. What have we established as our typical range of behaviors: How do we set up initial appointments, allocate our time, address new (and long-term) clients, ask to be addressed by our clients, handle no-shows, respond to late payments, engage in nonsexual touch, communicate with clients between sessions, and so on? Exploring our "usual" behaviors may reveal interesting patterns and implications.

---

[3]Stone, M. T. (1982). Turning points in therapy. In S. Slipp (Ed.), *Curative factors in dynamic psychotherapy* (pp. 259–279). New York: McGraw-Hill.

Advances in Theory, Research, and Practice

In whatever areas we specialize, with whatever populations, problems, and interventions we work, the relevant theory, research, and practices are constantly evolving. When stuck, it is almost always worth conducting a literature search or using some other means to find out whether there are new theoretical contributions, research findings, or practice innovations or guidelines that might be helpful in understanding how we arrived at an impasse, how we might find a way to move beyond it, and whether a possible intervention under consideration makes sense for this particular client and situation.

The Internet is a rich resource, especially for those without convenient access to a comprehensive professional library, for searching the literature. Abstracts of theoretical, research, practice, and review articles can be found on PsycINFO, Medline, and a variety of other databases. A collection of links to practice guidelines in the areas of assessment, therapy, counseling, and forensics can be found at http://kspope.com.

When reviewing other forms of the scientific and professional literature have not helped them respond to an impasse or decide whether to use a questionable intervention, some therapists have found it useful to read first-person accounts by therapists who have faced similar situations. Excerpts from several of these first-person accounts appear among the scenarios in chapter 6.

Looking for Logical Flaws

We may seem to have all the information we need about the client, the client's history, the client's condition, the relevant theory and research, and yet we're still caught in an impasse. It may not be the information and ideas that are the problem but the way we're putting them together. All of us are vulnerable to making mistakes in logic that can lead us astray. It may be helpful to go systematically through the logical fallacies discussed in chapter 1 to determine whether any play a role in creating the impasse.

The Legal and Ethical Framework

When caught in an impasse, it can be helpful to ensure that we're adequately aware of the relevant legal and ethical framework. The legislation and case law are constantly evolving, and a re-reading of the current professional ethics codes (e.g., the American Psychological Association's ethics code for psychologists, the National Association of Social Workers ethics code for social workers) when we experience a difficult impasse often brings unexpected insights and perspectives. These and other ethics codes and practice guidelines are on the Web and can be accessed at http://kspope.com/ethcodes/index.php.

Of course, the legal and ethical standards may be in conflict with each other or may not speak clearly to an issue. Moreover, even if the formal codes seem clear about a situation, the codes themselves should never replace thought.

> Awareness of the ethics codes is crucial to competence in the area of ethics, but the formal standards are not a substitute for an active, deliberative, and creative approach to fulfilling our ethical responsibilities. They prompt, guide, and inform our ethical consideration; they do not preclude or serve as a substitute for it. There is no way that the codes and principles can be effectively followed or applied in a rote, thoughtless manner. Each new client, whatever his or her similarities to previous clients, is a unique individual. Each situation also is unique and is likely to change significantly over time. The explicit codes and principles may designate many possible approaches as clearly unethical. They may identify with greater or lesser degrees of clarity the types of ethical concerns that are likely to be especially significant, but they cannot tell us how these concerns will manifest themselves in a particular clinical situation. They may set forth essential tasks that we must fulfill, but they cannot tell us how we can accomplish these tasks with a unique client facing unique problems. . . . There is no legitimate way to avoid these struggles. (p. 17)[4]

---

[4]Pope, K. S., & Vasquez, M. J. T. (1998). *Ethics in psychotherapy and counseling: A practical guide* (2nd ed.). San Francisco: Jossey-Bass.

When thinking through the ethics of a situation, we are always vulnerable to the cognitive strategies for justifying unethical behavior, outlined in chapter 1. It is always worth taking some time to consider whether we've put one or more of these strategies to work, which may have landed us in the impasse or block the exit routes.

Perhaps some of the most difficult deliberations involve conflicts between the law and the therapist's deepest values. Neither compliance with the law nor a choice to ignore the law in this instance seems an adequate response. The historic approach to breaking (what seems to the individual to be) an unjust law while simultaneously demonstrating respect for the principle of "no one above the law"—that is, "civil disobedience"—is often precluded to therapists in light of the nature of their work, as the following passage describes:

> Edmund Burke (1790/1961) stated the importance of absolute compliance with the law: "One of the first motives to civil society, and which becomes one of its fundamental rules, is that no man should be judge in his own cause" (p. 71). The U.S. Supreme Court, in *Walker V. Birmingham* (1967), underscored this "belief that in the fair administration of justice no man can be judge in his own case, however exalted his station, however righteous his motives, and irrespective of his race, color, politics, or religion" (pp. 1219–1220).
>
> Henry David Thoreau (1849/1960), however, urged that if a law "requires you to be the agent of injustice to another, then, I say, break the law" (p. 242). Even the California Supreme Court seemed to give tacit approval to breaking the law as long as it is done within the framework of civil disobedience: "If we were to deny to every person who has engaged in . . . nonviolent civil disobedience . . . the right to enter a licensed profession, we would deprive the community of the services of many highly qualified persons of the highest moral courage" (*Hallinan v. Committee of Bar Examiners of State Bar*, 1966, p. 239).
>
> Neither stance may seem acceptable to psychologists who believe that compliance with a legal or professional obligation would be harmful, unjust, or otherwise wrong. Absolute compliance connotes a "just following orders" mentality all

too ready to sacrifice personal values and client welfare to an imperfect system of rules and regulations. Selective noncompliance connotes an association of people who have anointed themselves as somehow above the law, able to pick and choose which legal obligations and recognized standards they will obey.

Civil disobedience itself may be precluded in significant areas of psychology. Coined as a term by Thoreau, civil disobedience as a concept has been developed, defined, and justified as an act involving open and public violation of the law while volunteering to accept the legal penalties (Gandhi, 1948; King, 1958, 1964; Plato, 1956a, 1956b; Thoreau, 1849/1960; Tolstoy, 1894/1951). This absolute openness—the lack of any attempt to avoid detection and prosecution—is essential in reaffirming respect for the process of law and accountability. But how can a psychologist, for example, publicly refuse to make a mandated report (e.g., regarding child abuse or potential harm to third parties) about a student, client, or subject without betraying the supposedly secret information? (p. 828)[5]

Continued Questioning

One of the most useful—perhaps necessary— steps when caught in a seemingly permanent impasse or considering whether to use a questionable intervention is to continue the process of questioning. This persistent questioning can, as previously mentioned, be viewed as a fundamentally important aspect of psychological science and practice. The *American Psychologist* article "Science as Careful Questioning," for example, emphasized a method designed "not to provide a simplified set of supposed answers or support a sense of certitude but rather to suggest that an essential task of psychologists is careful, informed, and comprehensive questioning" (p. 997).[6] Ethics is another area of our work in which continued questioning is key.

---

[5]Pope, K. S., & Bajt, T. R. (1988). When laws and values conflict: A dilemma for psychologists. *American Psychologist, 43,* 828; also available at http://kspope.com.

[6]Pope, K. S. (1997). Science as careful questioning: Are claims of a false memory syndrome epidemic based on empirical evidence? *American Psychologist, 52,* 997–

This book's approach is not to provide a simplified set of supposed answers, set forth an easy cookbook approach to the ethics of clinical work, or support a sense of certitude but rather to suggest that an essential task of clinical and counseling psychologists is this process of careful, informed, and comprehensive questioning. We must question our own assumptions, biases, and perspectives, not just once during initial training, but throughout our careers. We must also question claims about diagnoses, interventions, and the standard of care, no matter how prestigious or popular the source. (p. 71)[7]

Earlier steps might be characterized as directing our questioning toward what we don't know: What new advances in research, theory, or practice that we aren't yet aware of would a literature search uncover? Has there been a change in the relevant legislation or case law? What might we find out from a consultant that we don't already know? And it is useful for us to continue in this direction because few attain the status of genuine "know it all."

If the impasse persists, the questioning might also take another direction: toward what we know. Or at least what we think we know. The continued questioning of our most cherished beliefs, longstanding assumptions, basic approaches, sacred cows, popular views, and unquestionable certainties can sometimes lead us to the most unexpected discoveries and meaningful progress.

It is worth reminding ourselves of this important aspect of our identity as psychological scientists and practitioners: Whatever answers we have—or think we have—we are never without questions, and a willingness to pursue them wherever they lead.

1006; see also Pope, K. S. (1996). Memory, abuse, and science: Questioning claims about the false memory syndrome epidemic. Invited address for the American Psychological Association's Award for Distinguished Contributions to Public Service delivered at the 103rd Annual Convention of the American Psychological Association. *American Psychologist, 51,* 957–974. These articles are also available at http://kspope.com.
[7]See footnote 4, this chapter.

Appendix

Therapists' Anger, Hate, Fear, and Sexual Feelings: National Survey of Therapist Responses, Client Characteristics, Critical Events, Formal Complaints, and Training

Kenneth S. Pope and Barbara G. Tabachnick

Certain feelings—anger, hate, fear, and sexual attraction or arousal—may make many therapists uncomfortable, have been largely neglected in the research literature, and may not be adequately addressed in graduate training programs. The purpose of this article is to focus attention on these feelings and to present some relevant empirical data.

Anger and Hate

Although the early analytic view of countertransference encouraged exploration of the therapist's uncomfortable, negative, or taboo feelings, Winnicott (1949) pioneered the frank acknowledgment of a therapist's anger at and hatred of a patient. Illustrating his themes with what must have been difficult, perhaps coura-

This article is reprinted from "Therapists' Anger, Hate, Fear, and Sexual Feelings: National Survey of Therapist Responses, Client Characteristics, Critical Events, Formal Complaints, and Training," by K. S. Pope and B. G. Tabachnick, 1993, *Professional Psychology: Research and Practice, 24,* pp. 142–152. Copyright 1993 by the American Psychological Association.

geous self-disclosures, he wrote that therapists "must not deny hate that really exists" (p. 70). The denial of hate led to "therapy that is adapted to the needs of the therapist rather than to the needs of the patient" (Winnicott, 1949, 74).

Subsequent writers have explored the distinct but often inter-related feelings of anger and hate as they emerge with regard to such issues as child sex abuse (e.g., Boniello, 1990; MacCarthy, 1988), sexual assault of adults (e.g., Colao & Hunt, 1983), human immunodeficiency virus (HIV) or acquired immunodeficiency syndrome (AIDS; e.g., Boccellari & Dilley, 1989; Cummings, Rapaport, & Cummings, 1986), ethnicity (e.g., Calnek, 1970; Jackson, 1973), hospitalization for psychotherapeutic (e.g., Lakovics, 1985) or medical (e.g., Kucharski & Groves, 1976–77) reasons, the use of physical restraints in treatment settings (Hunter, 1989), and diagnostic labels such as borderline personality disorder (e.g., Nadelson, 1977; Reiser & Levenson, 1984).

The writings have tended to focus on three distinct themes. First, therapists may find it exceptionally difficult to acknowledge these feelings. As Boccellari and Dilley (1989) emphasized in their discussion of helping people who suffer from AIDS, "Negative or ambivalent feelings towards the patient, such as anger and resentment, can be particularly difficult for the caregiver to admit. Yet recognizing and accepting these feelings can result in a decrease in tension and feelings of guilt" (p. 197). Though sometimes hard to acknowledge, the occurrence of a wide range of such feelings among therapists is understandable; for example, working with those who face death through illness (e.g., people suffering from AIDS) can challenge the personal resources of even the most determined and committed caregiver (e.g., Trice, 1988).

Second, such feelings, when unacknowledged or inadequately addressed, may have devastating consequences. Reiser and Levenson (1984), for example, explore how diagnosing an individual as suffering from borderline personality disorder may in some instances fail to reflect accurately or even approximately the clinical status of the patient but instead serve to "express countertransference hate" (p. 1528).

Third, such feelings, when promptly acknowledged and adequately addressed, may, under certain circumstances, serve as a therapeutic resource. Epstein (1977), for example, described how certain patients may benefit from the therapist's appropriate expression of anger within a firm context of friendliness, warmth, and respect. "By recognizing this anger and hate, the [therapist] can be honest. By appropriate expression of the anger, the [therapist] enables the patient to see ego boundaries for him- or herself and the [therapist]" (Epstein, 1977, p. 442).

Despite such discussions, however, the profession lacks research to help understand the extent to which therapists experience these feelings and the contexts (e.g., patient characteristics and behaviors, critical events in therapy) in which such feelings may occur.

Fear

Perhaps the most extensive literature on therapist fear focuses on fear of assaults. A recent review noted that "violence and assaultive behavior were not considered major problems by psychiatrists until the mid and late 1960s."

The research has tended to address the risk (i.e., the incidence or prevalence of actual assaults) rather than the fear of attacks by patients. An early survey of 100 psychiatrists, psychologists, and social workers working in an urban setting found that virtually one fourth (24%) reported having been assaulted by at least one patient in the previous 1-year period (Whitman, Armao, & Dent, 1976). A study of 99 nurses at a Veterans Administration medical center found that only 20% had never been assaulted by a patient (Lanza, 1985). A recent survey of 750 psychologists found that over one third (39.9%) reported having suffered at least one violent attack by a patient (Guy, Brown, & Poelstra, 1990).

The literature discussing therapist fear has focused not only on attacks by patients (e.g., Atkinson, 1991; Carney, 1977; Lion & Pasternak, 1973; Madden, 1977) but also on malpractice suits[1] (e.g., Brodsky, 1988), reporting child abuse (e.g., Pollak & Levy, 1989), helping older patients (e.g., Martindale, 1989), helping people suffering from HIV or AIDS (e.g., Baer, Hall, Holm, & Koehler,

---

[1]In a general survey on a different topic, a large minority (45.9%) of psychologists reported "avoiding certain clients for fear of being sued" (Pope, Tabachnick, & Keith-Spiegel, 1987, p. 996).

1989; Cole & Adair, 1988; Goldblum & Moulton, 1989), and patient reactions to difficult or painful interpretations (e.g., Sinason, 1991). As with anger and hate, there are only meager research data about the extent to which therapists experience fear.

Sexual Feelings

As late as 1986, the topic of therapists' sexual attraction to their clients (distinct from but related to the topic of therapist–client sexual involvement) was absent from the nonpsychodynamic literature, nor were there any relevant research data (Pope, Keith-Spiegel, & Tabachnick, 1986). Research published that year revealed that "87% (95% of men, 76% of women) have been sexually attracted to their clients . . . and that . . . many (63%) feel guilty, anxious, or confused about the attraction" (Pope et al., 1986, p. 147).

The psychodynamic literature, however, has discussed the nature and occurrence of the therapist becoming sexually aroused during therapy sessions (e.g., Ganzarain & Buchele, 1986, 1988; Searles, 1959). Like Winnicott (1949), Searles illustrated his discussion with descriptions of his own experiences, emphasizing the difficulty of confronting his own responses (in this case, genital excitement during a therapy session): "I reacted to such feelings with considerable anxiety, guilt, and embarrassment" (1959, p. 183).

Therapists' Feelings, the Context, and Training

One facet of this survey is exploratory. It was designed to collect a broad range of baseline data about the degree to which therapists experience the kinds of feelings discussed in the previous sections, the contexts (e.g., client behaviors, therapist behaviors, and events in therapy) in which such feelings occur, and how therapists rate their graduate training with regard to these feelings.

A second facet involved specific research questions. Are such factors as therapist and client gender systematically related to

(a) concerns about and actual occurrences of client suicide, (b) concerns about and actual occurrences of client violence, and (c) noticing that a client is physically attractive? Do the feelings and contextual experiences reflect coherent, underlying factors? If so, are these factors systematically related to (a) sexual involvement in therapy, (b) formal complaints against therapists, and (c) therapists' ratings of their training?

Method

A letter, questionnaire, and stamped, addressed envelope (for returning the questionnaire) were mailed to 300 men and 300 women randomly selected from Divisions 12 (Clinical Psychology), 17 (Counseling Psychology), 29 (Psychotherapy), and 42 (Psychologists in Independent Practice) of the American Psychological Association (APA) as listed in the *Membership Register* (APA, 1991).

In addition to asking the participant's age, gender, and theoretical orientation, the questionnaire contained four parts. Part 1 ("Your Feelings or Reactions With Adult Clients") contained 24 examples of feelings that a therapist might experience (see Table 1 for questionnaire items). Part 2 ("Your Adult Clients' Behaviors or Events") contained 16 examples of client behaviors or events that might occur in therapy with an adult client. Part 3 ("Your Actions or Reactions With Adult Clients") contained 27 examples of therapist behaviors.

Participants were asked to indicate the extent to which they had experienced each of the 24 feelings, encountered each of the 16 client behaviors or events, and engaged in each of the 27 actions or reactions for adult female clients. They were asked to make similar ratings for adult male clients. The rating codes were 0 = never, 1 = rarely (i.e., with 1%–2% of their male or female clients), 2 = sometimes (3%–19%), 3 = often (20%–50%), and 4 = most (51%–100%). The rating system was designed to provide some adjustment for the relative numbers of female and male clients: Participants were asked to indicate the percentage of their female clients with regard to whom they had experienced various feelings, behaviors, events, actions, or reactions and were

Table 1

Percentage of Psychologists in Each Category (N = 285)

	Rating									
	Female clients					Male clients				
Item	0	1	2	3	4	0	1	2	3	4
Part 1: Your Feelings or Reactions With Adult Clients										
1. Feeling afraid that a client may commit suicide (97.2)	1.8	37.5	55.8	4.6	0.0	6.3	49.5	39.3	2.8	0.0
2. Feeling afraid that a client may physically attack you (82.8)	48.8	48.1	2.8	0.0	0.0	16.1	66.3	15.1	0.4	0.0
3. Feeling afraid that a client may physically attack a third party (89.1)	23.2	59.3	16.1	0.7	0.0	8.4	50.5	37.5	1.4	0.0
4. Feeling afraid that a client may be physically attacked by a third party (79.3)	19.6	36.1	37.9	5.6	0.0	31.6	48.8	15.1	0.7	0.0
5. Feeling afraid that a client may engage in unsafe sex (88.4)	9.5	23.9	44.6	19.6	1.8	9.8	19.6	45.3	20.0	2.5
6. Feeling afraid that a client may need clinical resources that are unavailable (86.0)	10.5	24.9	44.2	17.2	1.4	10.9	27.0	42.1	14.4	1.8
7. Feeling afraid because a client's condition gets suddenly or seriously worse (90.9)	7.4	44.9	43.9	2.5	0.0	8.8	46.0	39.6	2.1	0.0
8. Feeling afraid that your colleagues may be critical of your work with a client (88.1)	11.2	50.5	33.3	4.2	0.0	11.6	48.8	33.7	3.5	0.0
9. Feeling afraid that a client may file a formal complaint against you (66.0)	35.8	55.1	7.7	0.7	0.0	5.6	41.3	10.0	36.1	5.8
10. Feeling afraid to work with a client who is HIV-positive (26.7)	76.8	14.7	3.5	1.8	0.0	69.1	20.0	4.9	1.8	0.0
11. Feeling so afraid about a client that it affects your eating, sleeping, or concentration (53.3)	48.8	42.5	8.1	0.4	0.0	21.8	54.4	19.6	2.8	0.0
12. Feeling angry with a client because he or she is verbally abusive toward you (80.7)	32.8	45.4	20.1	1.0	0.0	21.8	54.4	19.6	2.8	0.0
13. Feeling angry with a client because of his or her behavior toward a third party (82.5)	18.9	48.1	30.9	1.4	0.0	17.5	42.1	35.8	2.1	0.0
14. Feeling angry with a client because of late or unpaid therapy bills (82.5)	17.2	42.8	33.7	4.9	0.0	6.6	43.6	18.7	23.4	5.8
15. Feeling angry with a client because he or she is uncooperative with you (89.8)	9.1	49.8	38.6	2.1	0.4	11.2	48.4	36.1	2.1	0.0
16. Feeling angry with a client because he or she contacts you too often (86.7)	11.2	49.8	34.4	3.9	0.0	27.0	52.6	17.5	0.4	0.0
17. Feeling angry with a client because he or she is often late for or misses sessions (87.0)	11.2	51.9	33.3	2.8	0.0	14.7	51.9	28.4	2.5	0.0
18. Feeling angry with a client because he or she terminates suddenly (78.2)	21.1	52.6	25.3	0.7	0.0	22.5	53.0	20.7	1.8	0.0
19. Feeling angry with a client because he or she makes a suicide threat or attempt (64.9)	33.7	50.9	13.0	1.8	0.0	43.9	42.5	9.5	1.4	0.0
20. Feeling angry with a client because he or she makes too many demands (87.4)	10.5	47.4	36.1	4.9	0.0	18.9	52.6	23.2	2.5	0.0
21. Feeling so angry with a client you do something you later regret (45.6)	55.8	39.3	3.9	0.4	0.0	57.5	36.8	3.2	0.4	0.0
22. Feeling hatred toward a client (31.2)	70.5	24.9	3.5	0.4	0.0	68.4	24.9	3.9	0.4	0.0
23. Feeling sexually attracted to a client (87.3)	32.6	34.4	30.9	1.1	0.4	43.5	39.6	13.0	0.7	0.0
24. Feeling sexually aroused while in the presence of a client (57.9)	52.3	36.8	10.5	0.4	0.0	62.1	29.1	5.3	0.0	0.0
Part 2: Your Adult Clients' Behaviors or Events										
25. A client commits suicide (28.8)	82.8	15.4	1.1	0.0	0.4	76.1	20.7	0.4	0.0	0.0
26. A client physically attacks you (18.9)	88.4	10.5	0.4	0.0	0.4	85.6	10.9	0.7	0.0	0.4
27. A client physically attacks a third party (60.7)	54.7	36.5	7.4	0.7	0.7	38.9	46.3	10.2	1.1	0.4
28. A client files a complaint (e.g., malpractice, ethics, licensing) against you (11.6)	92.3	6.7	0.4	0.0	0.4	90.9	6.0	0.4	0.0	0.4
29. A client hugs you (89.1)	9.1	37.2	40.7	11.6	1.4	27.4	46.7	17.5	5.3	1.4
30. A client kisses you (24.2)	76.8	21.1	1.4	0.4	0.0	89.5	7.4	0.4	0.0	0.0
31. A client flirts with you (87.0)	29.1	43.5	24.6	1.8	0.0	39.3	42.1	15.1	0.4	0.0

Item	0	1	2	3	4	0	1	2	3	4
32. A client tells you that he or she is sexually attracted to you (73.3)	36.5	45.6	14.4	2.8	0.4	50.9	33.0	12.3	1.1	0.0
33. During a session, a client strips down to his or her underwear (2.5)	98.9	1.1	0.0	0.0	0.0	95.4	1.8	0.4	0.0	0.0
34. During a session, a client is naked above the waist (2.5)	99.6	0.4	0.0	0.0	0.0	94.7	1.8	0.7	0.0	0.0
35. During a session, a client is naked below the waist (1.1)	99.6	0.4	0.0	0.0	0.0	96.1	1.1	0.0	0.0	0.0
36. A client touches his or her own genitals while in your presence (18.2)	93.7	5.6	0.7	0.0	0.0	80.0	15.4	2.1	0.0	0.0
37. A client touches your genitals (1.4)	98.9	1.1	0.0	0.0	0.0	97.2	0.4	0.4	0.4	0.0
38. A client seems to become sexually aroused while in your presence (48.4)	63.2	31.6	4.6	0.0	0.0	63.2	29.5	4.2	0.4	0.0
39. A client seems to have an orgasm while in your presence (3.2)	97.2	2.8	0.0	0.0	0.0	98.6	0.7	0.0	0.0	0.0
40. A client gives you a massage (1.8)	89.2	0.7	1.1	0.0	0.0	96.1	0.7	0.7	0.0	0.0

Part 3: Your Actions or Reactions With Adult Clients

Item	0	1	2	3	4	0	1	2	3	4
41. Avoiding treating a client because he or she is HIV-positive (4.2)	94.7	1.8	1.4	0.4	0.4	93.0	1.8	1.4	0.4	0.4
42. Telling a client that you are afraid of him or her (33.0)	84.6	15.1	0.4	0.0	0.0	66.0	30.2	1.8	0.0	0.0
43. Obtaining a weapon to protect yourself against a possible attack by a client (3.2)	99.3	0.7	0.0	0.0	0.0	94.7	3.2	0.0	0.0	0.0
44. Using a weapon to protect yourself against an attack by a client (0.4)	100.0	0.0	0.0	0.0	0.0	97.5	0.4	0.0	0.0	0.0
45. Summoning police or security personnel for your protection from a client (27.0)	88.4	10.9	0.4	0.0	0.0	72.6	24.2	1.1	0.0	0.0
46. Having fantasies reflecting fear that a client will physically attack you (50.9)	73.7	24.6	1.4	0.01	0.0	48.8	45.3	3.9	0.0	0.0
47. Telling a client that you are angry with him or her (77.9)	26.3	53.3	19.3	0.4	0.0	26.0	52.3	18.6	1.1	0.0
48. Raising your voice at a client because you are angry at him or her (57.2)	45.6	45.6	7.0	0.4	0.4	45.6	44.2	6.7	0.4	0.0
49. Having fantasies that reflect your anger at a client (63.5)	38.9	40.0	19.3	1.4	0.4	37.9	39.6	18.6	1.4	0.4
50. Telling a client that you care about him or her (91.9)	5.3	15.8	49.8	21.4	7.0	8.1	17.2	45.6	19.6	6.7
51. Holding a client's hand (60.4)	38.9	39.6	18.6	2.5	0.4	59.6	28.8	8.4	0.7	0.4
52. Hugging a client (81.1)	17.5	40.7	32.6	7.4	1.8	33.7	42.5	16.5	3.9	1.4
53. Kissing a client (5.6)	94.4	4.6	0.7	0.4	0.0	95.1	2.1	0.0	0.4	0.0
54. Lying down next to a client (0.4)	99.3	0.4	0.0	0.0	0.0	97.2	0.4	0.0	0.0	0.0
55. Lying on top of or underneath a client (0.4)	99.6	0.4	0.0	0.0	0.0	97.5	0.4	0.0	0.0	0.0
56. Cradling or otherwise holding a client in your lap (8.8)	90.5	7.7	1.1	0.4	0.0	94.0	2.5	0.7	0.0	0.0
57. Giving a massage to a client (2.8)	97.5	1.4	0.7	0.0	0.0	94.7	1.8	0.7	0.0	0.0
58. Flirting with a client (19.6)	85.3	13.4	1.1	0.0	0.0	86.7	9.1	1.4	0.0	0.0
59. Touching a client's genitals (0.0)	99.6	0.0	0.0	0.0	0.0	97.2	0.0	0.0	0.0	0.0
60. Experiencing an orgasm during a session (0.0)	100.0	0.0	0.0	0.0	0.0	97.5	0.0	0.0	0.0	0.0
61. Telling a sexual fantasy to a client (6.0)	95.1	4.2	0.4	0.4	0.0	92.6	4.6	0.4	0.0	0.0
62. Suggesting that a client tell you about his or her sexual fantasies (68.1)	32.6	29.7	31.6	7.0	1.8	31.9	28.8	28.1	7.0	1.8
63. Reassuring a client that having sexual feelings about a therapist is not uncommon (77.9)	27.7	31.6	27.0	11.2	2.5	33.0	31.9	22.8	7.7	2.1
64. Noticing that a client is physically attractive (95.8)	2.8	9.5	43.5	33.7	10.2	9.5	17.9	36.8	23.9	9.1
65. Telling a client that you find him or her physically attractive (38.9)	62.8	26.0	8.4	2.1	0.4	66.3	20.7	7.6	2.9	0.4
66. Telling a current client that you never engage in posttermination sex with clients (27.7)	75.4	14.4	5.3	2.1	1.8	79.3	10.5	3.9	1.4	1.8
67. Talking with a current client about sharing a sexual relationship after termination (2.1)	97.9	1.4	0.0	0.0	0.4	96.5	0.7	0.0	0.0	0.4

Note. Ratings are as follow: 0 = *never*, 1 = *rarely* (1%–2%), 2 = *sometimes* (3%–19%), 3 = *often* (20%–50%), 4 = *most* (51%–100%). Responses 0–4 sum to less than 100% due to missing data. Values in parentheses represent percentage of therapists responding *rarely* or more often, combined for female and male clients.

asked to indicate the percentages of their male clients with regard to whom they had had such experiences.

The fourth part of the questionnaire asked participants to rate their graduate training with regard to three topics (i.e., fear, anger, and sexual excitement) using the following ratings: virtually none, poor, adequate, good, or excellent.

Results

Characteristics of the Participants

Two hundred and eighty-five respondents (141 men, 141 women, and 3 who did not indicate gender) returned usable questionnaires. Respondents were almost equally divided between those who were 45 years old or under (140) and those who were over 45 (143), with two leaving this item blank.

Eighty-three (21.1%) respondents described their theoretical orientation as psychodynamic, 48 (16.6%) as eclectic, 35 (12.3%) as cognitive–behavioral, 15 (5.3%) as existential, 15 (5.3%) as interpersonal, 12 (4.2%) as systems, and 11 (3.9%) as behavioral. Thirty-four (11.9%) respondents listed diverse orientations that were grouped as "other," and 32 (11.2%) left this item blank.

Ratings of Feelings and Experiences

Table 1 shows participants' ratings for each of the 67 feelings and experiences with respect to female and male clients.

Client Suicide: Concerns and Occurrence

Therapist concerns with suicide were tested in a 2 × 2 × 2 mixed between-between-within-subjects multivariate analysis of variance (MANOVA) on fears that a client may commit suicide and a client actually committing suicide.[2] Independent variables were therapist and client gender (between and within factors, respectively) and training, derived as a median split on the sum of the

---

[2]Except where noted, all analyses were planned.

three training variables (evaluation of training with respect to fear, anger, and sex).

There was a significant multivariate effect of therapist gender, multivariate $F(2, 269) = 7.41, p < .05, \eta^2 = .05$. Although there was no difference expressed in fear of clients committing suicide, male therapists reported higher frequencies of clients actually committing suicide ($M = 0.30$ on a scale of 0 to 4) than did female therapists ($M = 0.12$), univariate $F(1, 270) = 14.36, (p < .025)$.

Client gender also affected suicide concerns, multivariate $F(2, 169) = 30.27, (p < .05, \eta^2 = .18)$, and showed small interaction effects with both therapist gender, multivariate $F(2, 169) = 5.16, (p < .05, \eta^2 = .04)$, and training, multivariate $F(2, 169) = 4.48 (p < .05, \eta^2 = .03)$. All effects relating to client gender were on fear of the client committing suicide. In general, there was greater fear for female clients ($M = 1.64$) than for male clients ($M = 1.39$). However, the discrepancy between fear of suicide for female and male clients was smaller for male therapists and for therapists who gave higher ratings to adequacy of their training.

Physical Attacks by Clients: Concerns and Occurrence

Therapist concerns with physical attacks were addressed in a parallel $2 \times 2 \times 2$ between-between-within-subjects MANOVA on four variables reflecting fears and experiences of clients attacking therapists and others: fear of client attacking the therapist, fear of client attacking a third party, actual attacks on the therapist, and actual attacks on a third party.

There were significant main effects of therapist gender, multivariate $F(4, 263) = 4.30 (p < .05, \eta^2 = .06)$, and client gender, multivariate $F(4, 263) = 60.46 (p < .05, \eta^2 = .48)$. Male therapists were more fearful that a client would attack a third party ($M = 1.26$) than were female therapists ($M = 1.02$), univariate $F(1, 266) = 12.06 (p < .01)$.

Univariate differences between male and female clients were noted on three of the four variables: fear of attack on the therapist, fear of attack on a third party, and actual attacks on third parties. Male clients engendered greater fear of attack on the therapist ($M = 1.01$) than did female clients ($M = 0.53$), univariate $F(1, 266) = 171.33 (p < .01)$. Male clients also engendered greater fear of attack on a third party ($M = 1.34$) than did female clients ($M = 0.94$), univariate $F(1, 266) = 109.15$ ($p < .01$). These latter fears seem understandable in that more attacks on a third party were reported for male clients (0.74) than for female clients (0.53), univariate $F(1, 266) = 34.18$ ($p < .01$). There were no statistically significant interactions.

Noticing That Clients Are Physically Attractive

A 2 × 2 mixed between-within-subjects analysis of variance (ANOVA) was performed on ratings of "noticing that a client is physically attractive." Independent variables were gender of therapist and gender of client. Although there was no statistically significant difference between the ratings of male and female therapists, client gender did make a difference, $F(1, 272) = 62.45$ ($p < .05$, partial $\eta^2 = .19$). On average, ratings for female clients were higher ($M = 2.40$) than for male clients ($M = 2.06$).

There was also a significant interaction between therapist and client gender in the ratings, $F(1, 272) = 74.02$ ($p < .05$, partial $\eta^2 = .21$). Female therapists noticed that male and female clients were attractive about equally often, whereas male therapists noticed that female clients were physically attractive more often than male clients.

Other Differences Due to Client Gender

A post hoc one-way within-subjects MANOVA explored differences between female and male clients in terms of several client and therapist experiences: telling the client the therapist finds him or her physically attractive, hugging or kissing a client, cradling a client in the therapist's lap, seeming to have a sexual orgasm in the presence of the therapist, holding hands, and flirting (multivariate $\alpha = .01$; univariate $\alpha = .0015$).

The multivariate effect of client gender was statistically significant, multivariate $F(7, 264) = 26.44$ ($\eta^2 = .41$). Women clients were more often the recipients of therapist hugging ($M = 1.35$) than were men ($M = 0.95$), univariate $F(1, 270) = 115.11$. They were also more likely to be cradled in the therapist's lap ($M = 0.11$) than were male clients ($M = 0.04$), univariate $F(1, 270) = 20.36$.

Finally, they were more likely to have their hands held ($M = 0.85$) than were men ($M = 0.48$), univariate $F(1, 270) = 124.98$.

Factor Analysis of Feelings and Experiences

Fifty-three of the experiences were subjected to a factor analysis.[3] A composite score for each item was formed by summing the responses with respect to male and female clients. The analysis was based on 213 cases; 69 cases were missing data on one or more items (5 of the therapists dealt with female clients exclusively). Three cases were identified as multivariate outliers ($p < .001$) and were omitted from analysis.[4]

The principal factor analysis with varimax rotation yielded four factors, accounting for 66% of the total variance in the ratings. All four factors were internally consistent and well defined by the variables; the lowest of the squared multiple correlations for factors from variables was .781. The reverse, however, was not true. As seen in Table 2, communalities tended to be low. With a cutoff of .45 for interpretation of a factor loading, 15 of the items loaded on the first factor, interpreted as anger. The second factor, interpreted as sexual material, was defined by seven items. Four variables defined the third factor, interpreted as warmth, and six variables loaded on the fourth factor, interpreted as physical fear. Table 2 shows only those 32 variables (of the 53 analyzed) that loaded on at least one factor. Twenty-one of the variables loaded on none.

---

[3]The remaining 14 behaviors were omitted from factor analysis because at least 95% of the responses to those items were "never." With so little variability, these items would not load on any factor, and attempts to include them created many outlying cases.

[4]The three outliers were men. One reported that most of his clients filed complaints, physically attacked him, and committed suicide, and probably miskeyed his responses. The second reported physical attacks sometimes by both male and female clients, massages sometimes given by both male and female clients, avoiding treating both male and female clients who are HIV-positive, and often kissing both male and female clients. The third outlier reported sometimes feeling angry with female clients who make suicide threats or attempts and rarely feeling so with male clients; sometimes he is given massages by female clients and rarely given them by male clients, while at the same time reporting no physical attacks by clients, no clients touching their own genitals, never avoiding treating clients who are HIV-positive, and never kissing a client.

Table 2
Factor Loadings, Communalities (η^2), and Percentage of Variance for Principal Factors or Extraction and Varimax Rotation

Item	Factor loading	η^2
Factor 1. Anger (% of varience = 5.91)		
17. Feeling angry with a client because he or she is often late or misses sessions	.67	.46
18. Feeling angry with a client because he or she terminates suddenly	.63	.40
12. Feeling angry with a client because he or she is verbally abusive toward you	.62	.49
13. Feeling angry with a client because of his or her behavior toward a third party	.60	.45
20. Feeling angry with a client because he or she makes too many demands	.58	.41
14. Feeling angry with a client because of late or unpaid therapy bills	.57	.34
15. Feeling angry with a client because he or she is uncooperative with you	.57	.36
22. Feeling hatred toward a client	.56	.40
8. Feeling afraid that your colleagues may be critical of your work with a client	.56	.34
21. Feeling so angry with a client you do something you later regret	.52	.29
49. Having fantasies that reflect your anger at a client	.51	.48
16. Feeling angry with a client because he or she contacts you too often	.48	.28
23. Feeling sexually attracted to a client	.47	.43
7. Feeling afraid because a client's condition gets suddenly or seriously worse	.46	.32
19. Feeling angry with a client because he or she makes a suicide threat or attempt	.45	.35
Factor 2. Sexual Material (% of variance = 4.46)		
32. A client tells you that he or she is sexually attracted to you	.69	.51
31. A client flirts with you	.67	.55
38. A client seems to become sexually aroused while in your presence	.66	.50
63. Reassuring a client that having sexual feelings about a therapist is not uncommon	.64	.43
62. Suggesting that a client tell you about his or her sexual fantasies	.61	.41
36. A client touches his or her own genitals while in your presence	.46	.24
49. Having fantasies that reflect your anger at a client	.45	.48
Factor 3. Warmth (% of variance = 3.36)		
52. Hugging a client	.81	.67
29. A client hugs you	.77	.62
50. Telling a client that you care about him or her	.61	.41
51. Holding a client's hand	.54	.32
Factor 4. Physical Fear (% of variance = 3.18)		
3. Feeling afraid that a client may physically attack a third party	.57	.38
45. Summoning police or security personnel for your protection from a client	.55	.33
2. Feeling afraid that a client may physically attack you	.50	.38
10. Feeling afraid to work with a client who is HIV-positive	.47	.29
27. A client physically attacks a third party	.47	.31
26. A client physically attacks you	.47	.31

of the factors. Only one item was complex, loading on both factors 1 and 2: having fantasies that reflect anger toward a client.

Feelings and Experiences Related to Demographic Variables

A 2 × 2 × 2 MANOVA was performed on the four factor scores as a function of gender, age group, and theoretical orientation (psychodynamic vs. all others). The only statistically significant effect was theoretical orientation, multivariate $F(4, 174) = 9.28$ ($p < .05$, $\eta^2 = .18$). Two of the four factors showed significant differences between psychodynamically oriented therapists and others: sexual material and warmth.

Psychodynamic therapists were more likely to experience the items in factor 2 (i.e., client flirting, client talking about sexual attraction to therapist, client touching his or her own genitals, client seeming to become sexually aroused, therapist having fantasies that reflect anger, therapist suggesting client tell about sexual fantasies and reassuring client about sexual feelings toward therapists) than were other therapists, univariate $F(1, 177) = 14.59$ ($p < .01$). For psychodynamically oriented therapists, the mean for the seven experiences was 1.85 (on a scale of 0 to 4), whereas the mean for the other therapists was 1.37.

Psychodynamically oriented therapists were less likely to experience items in factor 3 (i.e., hugging and being hugged by a client, holding a client's hand, and telling a client you care about her or him), univariate $F(1, 177) = 14.79$ ($p < .01$). The mean for psychodynamic therapists for those four items was 2.24, whereas the mean for the remaining therapists was 2.74.

Sexual Involvement in Therapy

Twenty-seven therapists (10 women and 17 men) were identified as experiencing sexual involvement in therapy.[5] Therapists were

---

[5]The term *sexual involvement in therapy* is used here *only* as a convenient summary label for the seven identified items; the term may have significantly different meanings or connotations when used elsewhere in the professional literature.

so defined if they answered anything other than "never" to questions about clients stripping to underwear, being naked above (female only) or below the waist, touching the therapists' genitals, therapists lying on top of or underneath a client, touching a client's genitals, telling a sexual fantasy to a client, or talking with a current client about sharing a sexual relationship after termination. A 2 × 2 × 2 logit analysis on sexual involvement by gender and age of therapist showed no statistically significant relation.

A one-way MANOVA was performed to investigate differences between therapists who were and were not identified as sexually involved in their factor scores on anger, fear, sexual material, and warmth; their evaluation of their graduate training in dealing with sexual excitement; and their experience of having clients file complaints against them.

There was a significant difference between the two groups, multivariate $F(6, 197) = 6.30$ ($p < .05$, $\eta^2 = .16$). Among the six dependent variables, each evaluated at $\alpha = .008$, complaints and sexual material showed differences between groups, univariate $F(1, 202) = 15.96$ and 12.80, respectively.

The average rating for "a client files a complaint . . . " for therapists identified as sexually involved was 0.5, whereas for remaining therapists the average was 0.11. Therapists who were identified as sexually involved also showed higher ratings ($M = 2.23$) on the items defining the factor labeled *sexual material* (see Table 2) than did other therapists ($M = 1.45$); this finding is not surprising in light of the shared items.

Complaints Against Therapists

Because the overall rate of complaints was less than 10% for either female or male clients, most analyses of complaints used a dichotomized variable in which therapists were divided into those who had never had a complaint filed and those who had. A 2 × 2 × 2 logit analysis of complaints by therapist gender and the dichotomized training variable (less than adequate, adequate or better) showed a significant relation between gender and complaints, $\chi^2(1, N = 281) = 7.63$ ($p < .05$). Although 17% of the male therapists had at least one complaint filed against them, only 6% of the female therapists did.

Table 3
Evaluation of Graduate Training in Regard to Fear, Anger, and Sexual Excitement

Item	Percentage rating				
	Virtually none	Poor	Adequate	Good	Excellent
Fear	22.8	23.9	24.6	17.2	8.1
Anger	13.3	24.2	23.2	22.8	13.0
Sexual excitement	27.0	23.2	19.6	14.7	10.9

Note. Responses sum to less than 100% due to missing data.

A one-way MANOVA was performed on scores for the four factors described in Table 2 as well as for experiences of client suicide. The independent variable was whether or not the therapist had a complaint filed. A significant multivariate relation was found, multivariate $F(5, 207) = 2.52$ ($p < .05$, $\eta^2 = .06$). The only variable significantly related to complaints was the factor score for physical fear, univariate $F(1, 211) = 7.22$ ($p < .01$). Therapists who had complaints filed against them were more fearful (mean of six variables contributing to factor 4 = 1.31) than were therapists who had never had complaints filed against them ($M = 1.01$).

To investigate the relation between complaints and client gender (a within-subjects variable), scores on complaints had to be treated as if continuous, despite the poor distribution. A one-way within-subjects ANOVA on complaints as a function of client gender showed no significant difference in complaints.

Evaluation of Training

Table 3 displays the responses to questions about the adequacy of graduate training programs in addressing fear, anger, and sexual excitement in therapy.

A post hoc one-way within-subjects ANOVA compared mean ratings on adequacy of three levels of training: anger, fear, and sexual excitement ($\alpha = .01$). The analysis showed that the difference in evaluation for the three types of training was statistically significant, $F(2, 540) = 27.00$ ($\eta^2 = .09$).

Ratings of training in the three areas showed strong positive correlations (i.e., the correlation between training ratings for fear and anger was .75, for fear and sex was .69, and for anger and sex was .66), but no statistically reliable relations emerged (at $\alpha =$

.004 to adjust for multiple testing) between evaluation of training and factor scores reflecting feelings and experiences in those areas.

A two-way MANOVA showed no differences in evaluation of graduate training in dealing with fear, anger, and sex as a function of theoretical orientation (psychodynamic vs. other) and age group. Neither age group nor theoretical orientation—either singly or in interaction—was reliably associated with evaluation of graduate training.

Discussion

Validity and Interpretation

Although participants were randomly selected from four APA divisions (12, 17, 29, and 42), the degree to which these results are genuinely representative of those divisions or of the close to 50,000 people (both APA and non-APA members) who are licensed to practice psychology (Dorken, Stapp, & VandenBos, 1986) is unknown.

Equally troublesome is the issue of self-report regarding sensitive topics, especially when some of the reporting involves retrospective evaluations—vulnerable to memory's imperfections (see Pope, 1990)—of training programs. As noted previously, research findings suggest that most psychologists may "feel guilty, anxious, or confused about [sexual] attraction [to clients]" (Pope et al., 1986, p. 147). For some, acknowledging to self or others that they have experienced such strongly negative feelings as "hate" toward those who have come to them for help may be extremely difficult, especially if their training has not encouraged them to recognize, accept, and examine such feelings. Prior research has demonstrated the extent to which "demand characteristics" (e.g., Barber, 1976; Orne, 1962) can influence research findings. More specifically, participants may tend to provide what they believe to be "socially approved" or "socially desirable" responses (e.g., Crowne & Marlowe, 1964; Edwards, 1982; Tanur, 1991).

Consequently, exceptional caution is warranted in interpreting these results, especially pending replication studies published in peer-reviewed journals. In light of such cautions and of space constraints, a few of the themes emerging from this survey are discussed in the following sections.

Feelings and Context

These findings suggest that therapists tend to experience fear, anger, and sexual feelings in the context of their work. Over 80% of the respondents reported experiencing each of the feelings—with nine exceptions—described in Part 1. The most widespread feeling was fear that a client would commit suicide, experienced by 97.2% of the participants (i.e., only one participant reported never feeling afraid that either a female or male client would commit suicide), followed by fear that a client would get worse (90.9%), anger at a client for being uncooperative (89.8%), and fear that a client will attack a third party (89.1%).

Participants reported that fear could exert debilitating effects on the therapist: Over half (53.3%) indicated having felt so afraid about a client that it affected their eating, sleeping, or concentration. Male clients engendered this type of debilitation for about 75% of the participants; about 50% of the therapists reported such fear with regard to female clients. Sometimes the fear focused (for more than 4 out of every 5 participants) on the lack of available clinical resources to meet a client's needs, sometimes (for 2 out of 3 participants) on the possibility that a client would file a complaint, and sometimes (for more than 4 out of 5 participants) on possible criticism by colleagues.

The least frequently reported feeling was fear of working with a client who was HIV-positive, reported by 20% of the respondents with regard to female clients and by 30.9% with regard to male clients. These findings are difficult to interpret because it is unclear whether those who did not report this fear were working with clients whom they knew to be infected with HIV. The second least frequently reported feeling was hatred, reported by slightly less than one third of the participants. Almost half (46%) reported feeling so angry with a client that they had done something that they later regretted. These were the only three items in Part 1 endorsed by less than half of the participants.

Over half (57.9%) of the participants reported experiencing sexual arousal while in the presence of a client. Almost half (47.7%)

of the participants reported becoming sexually aroused during therapy sessions with female clients, whereas about a third (34.4%) reported arousal with male clients. Eighty-seven percent of the participants reported at least some sexual attraction to clients, consistent with previously reported national rates of 86.8% (Pope et al., 1986) and 87.5% (Pope, Tabachnick, & Keith-Spiegel, 1987). About two thirds (66.8%) of the participants reported sexual attraction to female clients; about one half (53.3%) to male clients.

The factor analysis revealed that when feelings were examined in conjunction with the other survey items (e.g., therapist and client behaviors), four well-defined and internally consistent factors emerged: anger, sexual material, warmth, and physical fear. Not surprisingly, the feelings tended to be related to the contextual items: All four factors spanned more than one of the three major parts of the questionnaire: therapist feelings and reactions, clients' behaviors or events, and actions or reactions with clients. So, for example, factor 4 shows that therapists who are physically fearful are those who reportedly have reason to be so, for instance, having experienced clients who have physically attacked.

Patient Suicide and Violence

These findings illustrate the violent and potentially lethal behaviors (e.g., suicide, assaults) that therapists must confront in their work. Over 18% reported having been physically attacked by at least one client; 58% reported that a male patient had attacked a third party, whereas 44.6% reported that a female patient had attacked a third party. About one fourth of the participants reported having fantasies that a female client will attack them; one half reported such fantasies about a male client. About one tenth reported summoning police or security personnel for protection from a female client; about one fourth reported making such calls for protection from a male client. Less than 4% reported obtaining a weapon for protection against a client, and none reported using a weapon for protection.

Over one fourth (28.8%) indicated that they had experienced at least one client suicide. About one out of six participants reported at least one female patient who committed suicide; about one out of five reported at least one male patient who took his life. Male therapists reported higher frequencies of patient suicide than did female therapists, a finding that might (or might not) be due to differing clientele. It is interesting that therapists tended to be more concerned about the possibility of suicide by female patients in light of the research indicating that male patients tend to have higher suicide rates (e.g., Bongar, 1991).

These violent or self-destructive events are likely to have understandably traumatic consequences for the therapist (e.g., Atkinson, 1991; Brown, 1987; Carney, 1977; Chemtob, Bauer, Hamada, Pelowski, & Muraoka, 1989; Chemtob, Bauer, Hamada, Torigoe, & Kinney, 1988; Deutsch, 1984; Goldstein & Buongiorno, 1984; Henn, 1978; Lion & Pasternak, 1973; Madden, 1977). A study of 200 therapists who had recently lost a patient to suicide, for example, found not only intense feelings of grief, loss, and depression that anyone might experience after the death of someone he or she cared about but also feelings of guilt, inadequacy, self-blame, and fears of being sued, second-guessed, or scapegoated in the public press (Litman, 1965). A more recent study found that "trainees with patient suicides reported stress levels equivalent to that found in patient samples with bereavement and higher than that found with professional clinicians who had patient suicides" (Kleespies, Smith, & Becker, 1990, p. 257).

Attraction, Touching, Nudity, and Sexual Issues

Although clients' hugs, flirting, and statements of sexual attraction to the therapist are fairly frequent (over 50% of participants reported them for both female and male clients), clients' disrobing is exceptionally rare. Slightly over one third of the participants reported both male and female client (apparent) sexual arousal during sessions. Almost 3% of the participants reported that a female client seemed to have an orgasm while in the therapist's presence; 0.7% of participants reporting an apparent orgasm by a male client.

No participant reported touching a client's genitals or experiencing an orgasm during a session. Lying down on top of, next to, or underneath a client was exceedingly rare, as was giving a massage to a client. Over half reported hugging, over one fourth reported holding hands, and more than 1 in 10 reported flirting with regard to both female and male clients. Participants were also, according to their reports, more likely to notice that a female client is physically attractive. Some of these behaviors (e.g., hugging a client, kissing a client, client's disrobing) were explored in a prior survey, whose findings did not differ greatly from the current results (Pope et al., 1987).

The differential treatment of female clients is an important issue. In this survey, a higher percentage of female clients than male clients are noticed by their therapists as "physically attractive," are hugged by their therapists, and are cradled or held in their therapists' laps. Such differences may be largely due to cultural sex roles and socialization (e.g., Bernay & Cantor, 1986; Brown & Ballou, 1992; Gilbert, 1987; Gutek, Cohen, & Konrad, 1990; Gutek, Morash, & Cohen, 1983; Hare-Mustin & Marecek, 1990; Herman, 1992; Kabacoff, Marwit, & Orlofsky, 1985; Tavris, 1992). They may also be related to the tendency for therapist–patient sexual contact to involve a higher proportion of female patients (e.g., Bates & Brodsky, 1989; Gabbard, 1989; Holroyd, 1983; Noel & Watterson, 1992; see also Pope & Feldman-Summers, 1992; Pope & Vasquez, 1991) and for sexual involvement between psychology graduate students (many of whom are learning to be therapists) and their professors or supervisors to involve a higher proportion (adjusting for gender imbalances among faculty and among students) of female students (Glaser & Thorpe, 1986; Pope, Levenson, & Schover, 1979; Robinson & Reid, 1985; Vasquez, 1992), especially in light of a research finding that sexual involvement as a student with one's graduate professors or supervisors is statistically related to subsequent sexual involvement as a professional (Pope et al., 1979). Such issues are in need of more detailed research to enable a better understanding of the nature and consequences of differential treatment of women in professional relationships. Holroyd and Brodsky (1980), for example, pioneered this kind of research, finding that the differential treatment of female and male clients with regard to nonerotic touch was systematically related to therapist–patient erotic involvement.

Complaints

Over 1 out of 10 (11.6%) participants reported that at least one client had filed a complaint (e.g., malpractice, licensing, or ethics) against him or her. The findings suggest that male therapists are at significantly greater risk for such complaints: Almost three times as many male therapists (17%) as female therapists (6%) reported that at least one client filed a formal complaint (e.g., malpractice, ethics, or licensing) against them. Not surprisingly, therapists who indicated some form of sexual or quasisexual involvement (i.e., client strips to underwear, client being naked above [female only] or below the waist or touching the therapists' genitals, or therapist lying on top of or underneath a client, touching a client's genitals, telling a sexual fantasy to a client, or talking with a current client about sharing a sexual relationship after termination) had a complaint rating that was over four times as large as the rating for those who did not report such involvement (rating of 0.5 vs. 0.11; see item number 28 in Table 1).

Training

Graduate training with regard to feelings can span a diverse range of formats: formal classes, seminars, case conferences, practica, field placements, and clinical supervision as well as the less formal learning opportunities (Pope, Sonne, & Holroyd, 1993). Respondents were asked to provide an overall rating for their graduate training in this regard. A large percentage of participants rated their graduate training as inadequate (i.e., nonexistent or poor) with regard to anger, fear, and sexual arousal (41%, 50%, and 65%, respectively).[6] Previous theory and research (e.g., Pope et al., 1986; Searles, 1965; Winnicott, 1949) suggest that such feelings may make both therapists and students uncomfortable. To the extent that such discomfort may lead to neglect of these issues in training programs, therapists-in-training may lack the support to develop the knowledge, resources, confidence, and skills to acknowledge, accept, and understand such feelings when they occur in the therapist's work. Feelings such as anger, hate, fear, sexual attraction, and sexual arousal provide exceptional opportunities for teaching—and research—that, as suggested by these findings, may yet be largely untapped.

---

[6]That evaluations of training do not differ according to theoretical orientation is somewhat surprising in light of the psychodynamic therapies' long history of writings emphasizing countertransference.

In summary, the findings are a reminder of the intense, exciting, complex, stressful, and sometimes dangerous work that psychologists do, and that the responsibilities of that work are not the sort that can be carried out in an unfeeling manner. Acknowledging and trying to understand the feelings that come with the work may be an important part of the work itself.

References

American Psychological Association (APA). (1991). *APA membership register*. Washington, DC: Author.

Atkinson, J. C. (1991). Worker reaction to client assault. *Smith College Studies in Social Work, 62*, 34–42.

Baer, J. W., Hall, J. M., Holm, K., & Koehler, S. L. (1989). Treatment of people with AIDS on an inpatient psychiatric unit. In J. W. Dilley, C. Pies, & M. Helquist (Eds.), *Face to face: A guide to AIDS counseling* (pp. 175–185). San Francisco: AIDS Health Project, University of California, San Francisco.

Barber, T. X. (1976). *Pitfalls in human research*. Elmsford, NY: Pergamon Press.

Bates, C. M., & Brodsky, A. M. (1989). *Sex in the therapy hour: A case of professional incest*. New York: Guilford Press.

Bernay, T., & Cantor, D. W. (Eds.). (1986). *The psychology of today's woman: New psychoanalytic visions*. Hillsdale, NJ: Analytic Press.

Boccellari, A., & Dilley, J. W. (1989). Caring for patients with AIDS dementia. In J. W. Dilley, C. Pies, & M. Helquist (Eds.), *Face to face: A guide to AIDS counseling* (pp. 186–197). San Francisco: AIDS Health Project, University of California San Francisco.

Bongar, B. (1991). *The suicidal patient: Clinical and legal standards of care*. Washington, DC: American Psychological Association.

Boniello, M. (1990). Grieving sexual abuse: The therapist's process. *Clinical Social Work Journal, 18*, 367–379.

Brodsky, S. L. (1988). Fear of litigation in mental health professionals. *Criminal Justice and Behavior, 15*, 492–500.

Brown, H. N. (1987). The impact of suicide on therapists in training. *Comprehensive Psychiatry, 28*, 101–112.

Brown, L. S., & Ballou, M. (Eds.). (1992). *Personality and psychopathology: Feminist reappraisals*. New York: Guilford Press.

Calnek, M. (1970). Racial factors in the countertransference: The black therapist and the black client. *American Journal of Orthopsychiatry, 40*, 39–46.

Carney, F. L. (1977). Outpatient treatment of the aggressive offender. *American Journal of Psychotherapy, 31*, 265–274.

Chemtob, C. M., Bauer, G. B., Hamada, R. S., Pelowski, S. R., & Muraoka, M. Y. (1989). Patient suicide: Occupational hazard for psychologists and psychiatrists. *Professional Psychology: Research and Practice, 20*, 294–300.

Chemtob, C. M., Bauer, G. B., Hamada, R. S., Torigoe, R. Y., & Kinney, B. (1988). Patient suicide: Frequency and impact on psychologists. *Professional Psychology: Research and Practice, 19*, 421–425.

Colao, F., & Hunt, M. (1983). Therapists coping with sexual assault. *Women & Therapy, 2*, 205–214.

Cole, J. (Producer), & Adair, P. (Director). (1988). *Facing our fears: Mental health professionals speak* [Motion picture]. San Francisco: AIDS Health Project, University of California, San Francisco.

Crowne, D. P., & Marlowe, D. (1964). *The approval motive: Studies in evaluative dependence.* New York: Wiley.

Cummings, M. A., Rapaport, M., & Cummings, K. L. (1986). A psychiatric staff response to acquired immune deficiency syndrome. *American Journal of Psychiatry, 143*, 682.

Deutsch, C. J. (1984). Self-report sources of stress among psychotherapists. *Professional Psychology: Research and Practice, 15*, 833–845.

Dorken, H., Stapp, J., & VandenBos, G. R. (1986). Licensed psychologists: A decade of major growth. In H. Dorken (Ed.), *Professional psychology in transition* (pp. 3–19). San Francisco: Jossey-Bass.

Edwards, A. L. (1982). *The social desirability variable in personality assessment and research.* New York: Greenwood.

Epstein, L. (1977). The therapeutic function of hate in the counter-transference. *Contemporary Psychoanalysis, 13*, 442–461.

Gabbard, G. O. (Ed.). (1989). *Sexual exploitation in professional relationships.* Washington, DC: American Psychiatric Press.

Ganzarain, R., & Buchele, B. (1986). Countertransference when incest is the problem. *International Journal of Group Psychotherapy, 36*, 549–566.

Ganzarain, R., & Buchele, B. (1988). *Fugitives of incest: A perspective from psychoanalysis and groups.* New York: New York Universities Press.

Gilbert, L. A. (1987). Sex, gender, and psychotherapy. In J. R. McNarmara & M. A. Appel (Eds.), *Critical issues, developments, and trends in professonal psychology* (Vol. 3, pp. 30–54). New York: Praeger.

Glaser, R. D., & Thorpe, J. S. (1986). Unethical intimacy: A survey of sexual contact and advances between psychology educators and female graduate students. *American Psychologist, 41*, 43–51.

Goldblum, P. B., & Moulton, J. (1989). HIV disease and suicide. In J. W. Dilley, C. Pies, & M. Helquist (Eds.), *Face to face: A guide to AIDS counseling* (pp. 152–164). San Francisco: AIDS Health Project, University of California, San Francisco.

Goldstein, L. S., & Buongiorno, P. A. (1984). Psychotherapists as suicide survivors. *American Journal of Psychotherapy, 38*, 392–398.

Gutek, B. A., Cohen, A. G., & Konrad, A. M. (1990). Predicting social–sexual behavior at work: A contact hypothesis. *Academy of Management Journal, 33*, 560–577.

Gutek, B. A., Morash, B., & Cohen, A. (1983). Interpreting social–sexual behavior in the work setting. *Journal of Vocational Behavior, 22*, 30–48.

Guy, J. D., Brown, C. K., & Poelstra, P. L. (1990). Who gets attacked? A national survey of patient violence directed at psychologists in clinical practice. *Professional Psychology: Research and Practice, 21*, 493–495.

Hare-Mustin, R. T., & Marecek, J. (Eds.). (1990). *Making a difference: Psychology and the construction of gender*. New Haven, CT: Yale University Press.

Henn, R. F. (1978). Patient suicide as a part of psychiatric residency. *American Journal of Psychiatry, 135*, 745–746.

Herman, J. L. (1992). *Trauma and recovery*. New York: Basic Books.

Holroyd, J. C. (1983). Erotic contact as an instance of sex-biased therapy. In J. Murrary & P. R. Abramson (Eds.), *Bias in psychotherapy* (pp. 285–308). New York: Praeger.

Holroyd, J. C., & Brodsky, A. M. (1980). Does touching patients lead to sexual intercourse? *Professional Psychology, 11*, 807–811.

Hunter, D. S. (1989). The use of physical restraint in managing out-of-control behavior in youth: A frontline perspective. *Child and Youth Care Quarterly, 18*, 141–154.

Jackson, A. M. (1973). Psychotherapy: Factors associated with the race of the therapist. *Psychotherapy: Theory, Research, and Practice, 10*, 273–277.

Kabacoff, R. I., Marwit, S. J., & Orlofsky, J. L. (1985). Correlates of sex role stereotyping among mental health professionals. *Professional Psychology: Research and Practice, 16*, 98–105.

Kleespies, P. M., Smith, M. R., & Becker, B. R. (1990). Psychology interns as patient suicide survivors: Incidence, impact, and recovery. *Professional Psychology: Research and Practice, 21*, 257–263.

Kucharski, A., & Groves, J. E. (1976–77). The so-called inappropriate psychiatric consultation request on a medical or surgical ward. *International Journal of Psychiatry in Medicine, 7*, 209–220.

Lakovics, M. (1985). A classification of countertransference phenomena and its application to inpatient psychiatry. *Psychiatric Journal of the University of Ottawa, 10*, 132–138.

Lanza, M. L. (1985). How nurses react to patient assault. *Journal of Psychosocial Nursing and Mental Health Services, 23*, 6–11.

Lion, J. R., & Pasternak, S. A. (1973). Countertransference reactions to violent patients. *American Journal of Psychiatry, 130*, 207–210.

Litman, R. E. (1965). When patients commit suicide. *American Journal of Psychotherapy, 19*, 570–583.

MacCarthy, B. (1988). Are incest victims hated? *Psychoanalytic Psychotherapy, 3*, 113–120.

Madden, D. J. (1977). Voluntary and involuntary treatment of aggressive patients. *American Journal of Psychiatry, 134*, 553–555.

Martindale, B. (1989). Becoming dependent again: The fears of some elderly persons and their younger therapists. *Psychoanalytic Psychotherapy, 4*, 67–75.

Nadelson, T. (1977). Borderline rage and the therapist's response. *American Journal of Psychiatry, 134*, 748–751.

Noel, B., & Watterson, K. (1992). *You must be dreaming*. New York: Poseidon.

Orne, M. T. (1962). On the social psychology of the psychological experiment: With particular reference to demand characteristics and their implications. *American Psychologist, 17*, 776–783.

Pollak, J., & Levy, S. (1989). Countertransference and failure to report child abuse and neglect. *Child Abuse and Neglect, 13*, 515–522.

Pope, K. S. (1990). Therapist–patient sexual involvement: A review of the research. *Clinical Psychology Review, 10*, 477–490.

Pope, K. S., & Feldman-Summers, S. (1992). National survey of psychologists' sexual and physical abuse history and their evaluation of training and competence in these areas. *Professional Psychology: Research and Practice, 23*, 353–361.

Pope, K. S., Levenson, H., & Schover, L. R. (1979). Sexual intimacy in psychology training: Results and implications of a national survey. *American Psychologist, 34*, 682–689.

Pope, K. S., Keith-Spiegel, P., & Tabachnick, B. G. (1986). Sexual attraction to clients: The human therapist and the (sometimes) inhuman training system. *American Psychologist, 41*, 147–158.

Pope, K. S., Sonne, J. L., & Holroyd, J. (1993). *Sexual feelings in psychotherapy: Explorations for therapists and therapists-in-training*. Washington, DC: American Psychological Association.

Pope, K. S., Tabachnick, B. G., & Keith-Spiegel, P. (1987). Ethics of practice: The beliefs and behaviors of psychologists as therapists. *American Psychologist, 42*, 993–1006.

Pope, K. S., & Vasquez, M. J. T. (1991). *Ethics in psychotherapy and counseling: A practical guide for psychologists*. San Francisco: Jossey-Bass.

Reiser, D. E., & Levenson, H. (1984). Abuses of the borderline diagnosis: A clinical problem with teaching opportunities. *American Journal of Psychiatry, 141*, 1528–1532.

Robinson, W. L., & Reid, P. T. (1985). Sexual intimacies in psychology revisited. *Professional Psychology: Research and Practice, 16*, 512–520.

Rosenbaum, M. (1991). Violence in psychiatric wards: Role of the lax milieu. *General Hospital Psychiatry, 13*, 115–121.

Searles, H. F. (1959). Oedipal love in the countertransference. *International Journal of Psychoanalysis, 40*, 180–190.

Sinason, V. (1991). Interpretations that feel horrible to make and a theoretical unicorn. *Journal of Child Psychiatry, 17*, 11–24.

Tanur, J. M. (Ed.). (1991). *Questions about questions: Inquiries into the cognitive bases of surveys*. Beverly Hills, CA: Russell Sage.

Tavris, C. (1992). *The mismeasure of woman*. New York: Simon & Schuster.

Trice, A. D. (1988). Posttraumatic stress syndrome-like symptoms among AIDS caregivers. *Psychological Reports, 63*, 656–658.

Vasquez, M. J. T. (1992). Psychologist as clinical supervisor: Promoting ethical practice. *Professional Psychology: Research and Practice, 23*, 196–202.

Whitman, R. M., Armao, B. B., & Dent, O. B. (1976). Assault on the therapist. *American Journal of Psychiatry, 133*, 426–429.

Winnicott, D. W. (1949). Hate in the counter-transference. *International Journal of Psychoanalysis, 30*, 69–74.

Index

About the Authors

Kenneth S. Pope, PhD, ABPP, received graduate degrees from Harvard and Yale and has been in independent practice as a licensed psychologist since the mid-1980s. A diplomate in clinical psychology, he has authored or coauthored more than 100 articles and chapters in peer-reviewed scientific and professional journals and books. He was elected a charter fellow of the American Psychological Society and a fellow of American Psychological Association (APA) Divisions 1, 2, 12, 29, 35, 41, 42, 44, and 51.

On the basis of his research in the 1970s on therapist–patient sex, he cofounded the University of California at Los Angeles (UCLA) Post-Therapy Support Program, the first center offering services, conducting research, and providing university-based training for graduate students and therapists seeking to work with people who had been sexually exploited by therapists. Ken taught courses in psychological and neuropsychological assessment, abnormal psychology, and professional standards of care at UCLA, where he served as a psychotherapy supervisor. He chaired the ethics committees of the APA and the American Board of Professional Psychology.

In the early 1980s, Ken was the director of clinical programs for a consortium of community mental health centers and hospitals. Drawing on his years of experience in the late 1960s and early 1970s as a full-time community organizer living in an inner-city area of severe poverty, he worked with the community, the hospitals, and the centers to find ways to meet community needs in accordance with its own cultures and ecology. By the end of his work in those areas, their programs included homebound services (in which therapists and others go to the homes of people whose chronic or terminal illnesses or disabilities prevent them from traveling), legal services for people who are poor or homeless, Manos de Esperanza (serving people whose primary language is Spanish), a 24-hour crisis service, peer-support services, and group homes that allow people who are mentally disabled to live independently.

His publications include 10 articles in *American Psychologist* and 11 books (such as *Ethics in Psychotherapy and Counseling*, 2nd edition, with Melba Vasquez; *The MMPI, MMPI–2, and MMPI–A in Court: A Practical Guide for Expert Witnesses and Attorneys*, 3rd edition, with James Butcher and Joyce Seelen; *Sexual Involvement With Patients: Patient Assessment, Subsequent Therapy, Forensics*; *The Stream of Consciousness: Scientific Investigations Into the Flow of Human Experience*, with Jerome Singer; *Law and Mental Health Professionals: California*, with Brandt Caudill; and *Surviving and Thriving as a Therapist: Information, Ideas, and Resources for Psychologists*, with Melba Vasquez).

One of his main interests is the family of special-needs dogs and cats who live in his home and whose photos and stories can be seen at http://kenpope.com. He also maintains three other Web sites: *Articles, Research, & Resources in Psychology* at http://kspope.com; *Accessibility & Disability Information & Resources in Psychology Training & Practice* at http://kpope.com; and *Resources for Companion Animals, Assistance Animals, & Special-Needs Animals* at http://catanddoghelp.com.

He provides a free psychology news service for about 1,000 psychologists, attorneys, psychiatrists, and others (anyone is welcome to join the mailing list). Each day he e-mails three to six messages, including excerpts from new and in-press articles in scientific and professional journals and from psychology-related articles from that morning's newspapers, job announcements, requests for information and resources from list members, and so on.

Ken received the Belle Mayer Bromberg Award for Literature; the Frances Mosseker Award for Fiction; the APA Division 42 Presidential Citation "In Recognition of His Voluntary Contributions, His Generosity of Time, the Sharing of His Caring Spirit [and] His Personal Resources"; the APA Division 44 Citation of Appreciation; the APA Division 12 Award for Distinguished Professional Contributions to Clinical Psychology; and the APA Award for Distinguished Contributions to Public Service, which includes the following citation:

> For rigorous empirical research, landmark articles and books, courageous leadership, fostering the careers of others, and

making services available to those with no means to pay. His works include 9 books and over 100 other publications on topics ranging from treating victims of torture to psychometrics to memory to ethics. His pioneering research has increased our understanding of therapist–patient sex, especially in the areas of effects on patients, tendencies to deny or discount risks, factors enabling known perpetrators to continue or resume not only practicing but also abusing patients, and approaches to prevention. As the title—*What Therapists Don't Talk About and Why*—of his acceptance talk for the Division 12 Award for Distinguished Professional Contributions to Clinical Psychology suggests, Pope's research frequently addresses concerns that are relatively neglected because they tend to cause anxiety, such as therapists' feelings of anger, hate, fear, or sexual attraction toward patients, or therapists' own histories of sexual and physical abuse. He frequently declines compensation for his work to advance psychology in the public interest. This is evident in his recent book, *Sexual Involvement With Therapists: Patient Assessment, Subsequent Therapy, Forensics*, published by the American Psychological Association. Pope waived all royalties for the volume in order that it might be sold at reduced price and be more readily available and useful. His integrity, good will, humor, and tireless work in the public interest represent the finest ideals of our profession. (p. 241)[1]

Janet L. Sonne, PhD, is a licensed psychologist in independent clinical and forensic practice in Redlands, California. She received her bachelor's degree in psychology from Stanford University, her master's degree in social and personality psychology from the University of California at Santa Barbara, and her doctorate in clinical psychology from UCLA. She was a founding psychologist of the graduate clinical psychology program at Loma Linda University; she recently retired from her position there as professor of psychology and director of clinical training. Previously, she was a member of the faculty of the Department of Psychiatry at Loma Linda University Medical School where she taught and supervised the psychotherapy training of psychiatry residents.

---

[1]American Psychological Association award for distinguished contributions to public service. (1995). *American Psychologist, 50,* 241–243.

In addition, she taught graduate students in departments of medicine, nursing, social work, and marriage and family therapy. She is former chair and member of the California Psychological Association Ethics Committee. She served twice as a member of the American Psychological Association (APA) Ethics Committee. She is an expert consultant to the California Board of Psychology, Board of Behavioral Science Examiners, and Board of Nursing, as well as to attorneys and religious organizations, regarding professional standard of care and competency issues and perpetration and sequelae of childhood sexual abuse. She is the author of several publications on the topic of therapist–patient relationships, including the book coauthored with Ken Pope and Jean Holroyd, *Sexual Feelings in Psychotherapy: Explorations for Therapists and Therapists-in-Training.*

Janet's interest in the intricacies of the ethical practice of psychotherapy began at Stanford in her first psychology course. Phil Zimbardo taught the course and ignited her fascination with how people make decisions to behave in altruistic versus self-serving ways toward others. While at UCLA, she participated with Ken Pope and Jackie Bouhoutsos in the Post-Therapy Support Group project, an innovative group therapy program for individuals who have experienced sexual intimacies with their therapists. Observing firsthand the complex underlying dynamics and powerfully negative effects of such experiences fanned Janet's dedication to research and intervention with the patients as well as with the therapist perpetrators. Her experiences on the California Psychological Association and the APA Ethics Committees and with various professional licensing boards have enhanced her appreciation of the importance of training mental health professionals to conceptualize ethical practice as a process of decision making rather than a set of rules.

Beverly Greene, PhD, ABPP, is a professor of psychology at St. John's University in Jamaica, New York, and a practicing clinical psychologist in independent practice in Brooklyn, New York. In honor of outstanding and significant contributions to psychology, she is a fellow of the American Psychological Association (APA) Divisions 9, 12, 29, 35, 42, 44, and 45; the Academy of Clinical Psychology; and the American Orthopsychiatric Association.

Dr. Greene holds a diplomate in clinical psychology from the American Board of Professional Psychology and is licensed as a psychologist in New York and New Jersey.

Dr. Greene received her bachelor's degree in psychology from New York University where she was a member of the first group of Martin Luther King Scholars. She completed her master's and doctor of philosophy degrees in clinical psychology at the Derner Institute of Advanced Psychological Studies of Adelphi University in Garden City, New York. She has served as a school psychologist with the New York City Board of Education and as a clinical assistant professor of psychiatry and director of inpatient child and adolescent psychology at King's County Hospital's Inpatient Child and Adolescent Psychiatry service in Brooklyn, New York. She has also served as a supervising psychologist and clinical assistant professor of child psychiatry at the University of Medicine and Dentistry's Community Mental Health Center in Newark, New Jersey. After a decade of work in public mental health, Dr. Greene joined the faculty of St. John's University in 1991 as a clinical associate professor. In 1995, she was granted tenure and promoted to the rank of full professor.

Dr. Greene has received numerous awards for distinguished senior career contributions. In 1996, she received the Outstanding Leadership Citation from APA's Committee on Lesbian, Gay, and Bisexual Concerns, citing her "elegant and groudbreaking research on mental health issues of African American lesbians" and long-standing education and training that cases the burdens of stigma, stereotype, and ignorance for sexual minorities and people of color. In 2000, she was honored with the APA Society for the Psychology of Women's Heritage award for "impressive and substantial scholarly contributions to the psychological literature highlighting critical issues on the psychology of women, on underrepresented groups of women, and in recognition of creative and innovative publications on the links between gender, ethnicity, and sexual orientation that serve to advance the understanding of the psychology of women." In 2003, she received the APA Committee on Women in Psychology's Distinguished Leadership Award for her long-standing career influence on women's issues and status, recognition as a leader whose contributions and scope of influence advance knowledge, foster understanding of women's lives, and improve the status of women and underrepresented subpopulations of women in psychology and in society. Specifically cited were her "profound and far-reaching contributions to psychological theory and practice relating to women, giving voice to the invisible and unheard."

Dr. Greene serves on the editorial and advisory boards of numerous scholarly journals, as well as in various positions of APA governance. She was a founding coeditor of the APA Society for the Psychological Study of Lesbian, Gay, and Bisexual Issues Series, *Psychological Perspectives on Lesbian, Gay, and Bisexual Issues*, and is the sole editor of volume 3, *Ethnic and Cultural Diversity Among Lesbians and Gay Men*. The author of more than 75 professional publications, she has received nine national awards for outstanding and significant scholarly contributions to the psychological literature. She is the recipient of the Association for Women in Psychology's 1991, 1995, and 2000 Women of Color Psychologies Award for publications that were deemed significant contributions to the development of greater understandings of the psychologies of women of color. Dr. Greene also received that association's Distinguished Publication Award in 1995 (for *Women of Color: Integrating Ethnic and Gender Identities in Psychotherapy*) and 2001(for *Psychotherapy With African American Women: Innovations in Psychodynamic Perspectives and Practice*) for significant and substantial scholarly contributions of research and theory that advance our understanding of the psychology of women. She also received the APA Society for the Psychology of Women's Psychotherapy With Women Research Award in 1995 and 1996. In 2000, two of her papers tied for this award, which is given annually for a paper judged on the basis of scholastic vigor, clinical impact, theoretical creativity and innovation, methodological skill, and clarity and style of presentation in addition to the judged importance to psychotherapy with women. The winning paper is recognized as a substantial and outstanding scholarly contribution to the theory, practice, and research of psychotherapy with women and as an innovative work that advances skills in psychotherapeutic work with women. The Georgia State Psychological Association honored Dr. Greene in 2000 for outstanding contributions to research on human sexual orientation. The Feminist Therapy Institute honored her with its 2002 Founding Foremothers award for outstanding contributions to the development of feminist psychology and psychotherapy theory.

In addition to awards for publications, she has received the APA Society for Clinical Psychology's 2000 MENTOR award for outstanding contributions and commitment to the teaching and training of clinical psychologists to deliver services to ethnic minority populations more effectively and its 2000 Psychology of Women mentor award for a psychologist who substantially aids women in clinical psychology to succeed at critical periods in their careers.

Recent honors include the 2004 Distinguished Career Contributions to Ethnic Minority Research Award sponsored by the APA Society for the Psychological Study of Ethnic Minority Issues in recognition of a senior person who has made significant contributions in writing, publishing, and disseminating information on ethnic minority populations and issues and thereby substantively contributed to the current understanding of ethnic minorities. The 2005 recipient of the APA Society for Clinical Psychology's Stanley Sue Award for Distinguished Professional Contributions to Diversity in Clinical Psychology, she is also the recipient of the Teacher's College, Columbia University 2006 Cross Cultural Roundtable's 16th Annual Janet Helms Award for Scholarship and Mentoring. Current projects include a collection of narratives, *A Minyan of Women: Family Dynamics, Jewish Identities and Psychotherapy Practice; Teaching Cultural Competence in Mental Health: A Handbook for Instructors;* and *Phenomenal Women: Psychological Vulnerability and Resilience Among High Achieving Black Women.*